CLAIMING PLACE

CLAIMING
PLACE

Biracial Young Adults of the
Post–Civil Rights Era

MARION KILSON

BERGIN & GARVEY
Westport, Connecticut • London

Library of Congress Cataloging-in-Publication Data

Kilson, Marion, 1936–
    Claiming place : biracial young adults of the post-civil rights era /
Marion Kilson.
        p. cm.
    Includes bibliographical references and index.
    ISBN 0–89789–760–9 (alk. paper)
        1. Racially mixed people—United States—Race identity.   2. Racially mixed
people—United States—Social conditions—20th century.   3. Young
adults—United States—Social conditions—20th century.   4. United
States—Race relations.   I. Title.
    E184.A1 K45   2001
    305.8'00973—dc21   00–031203

British Library Cataloguing in Publication Data is available.

Library of Congress Catalog Card Number: 00–031203
ISBN: 0–89789–760–9

First published in 2001

Bergin & Garvey, 88 Post Road West, Westport, CT 06881
An imprint of Greenwood Publishing Group, Inc.
www.greenwood.com

Printed in the United States of America

The paper used in this book complies with the
Permanent Paper Standard issued by the National
Information Standards Organization (Z39.48–1984).

10 9 8 7 6 5 4 3 2

For
Martin, Jennifer, Peter, and Hannah

Contents

Tables

Preface

For more than four decades I have lived in a Biracial world. As a professional European American woman, I am not always visible as a participant in this world. When I am alone among strangers, my Biracial affiliations are invisible. I, therefore, enjoy the privileges of Whiteness in public places. When I am with my husband, children, or grandchildren, my Biracial connections become visible. These ties are also considered when I am among friends or colleagues who are aware that my husband is African American and my children are Biracial.

Race and ethnicity have always been central to my domestic discourse and confronting racism part of quotidian life. Yet until the past decade, Biraciality has been existentially central but not the focus of domestic discourse. Wishing to learn more about my children's experiences as Biracial Americans and to discover how their experiences compared to other first-generation Biracial Americans of the post–Civil Rights era, I embarked on the research for *Claiming Place*.

Claiming Place has come into being through the generosity of many individuals and institutions. In the initial research phase, my daughters, Hannah Kilson-Kuchtic and Jennifer Kilson-Page, helped to frame the questions that I eventually posed to fifty other young adult Biracial Americans; they and various friends and colleagues told me about potential project participants. For assistance in the search for project participants, I am especially grateful to George C. Bond and to the individuals whom I interviewed who told me of their Biracial siblings, spouses, and friends and how I might find them. Although I wish that I could acknowledge by name the fifty-two men and women who shared some of their memories and perceptions of their Biracial experiences with me, I promised them confidentiality at the time of our conversations. Needless to say, without their generous assistance, this book could not be. I am enormously grateful to them for their candor and courage.

The second phase in the gestation of *Claiming Place* was the exhibition, "Claiming Place: Biracial American Portraits." With support from the Massachusetts Cultural Council, my colleagues, documentary photographer Max Belcher and designer Theresa Monaco and I created this traveling exhibition, which combined visual and verbal portraits of nineteen project participants. The exhibition appeared at six venues in Massachusetts between 1995 and 1997: Emmanuel College in Boston, Holyoke State Heritage Park, Fall River State Heritage Park, Salem State College, Cambridge Arts Council's Gallery 57, and Boston College. At the public forums introducing the show in Boston, Holyoke, and Salem, Professor George C. Bond of Columbia University, Dr. Ann Murray of Salem State College and I made presentations on changing conceptions of race, multicultural education, and themes in the Biracial American experience. Designed by Professor Theresa Monaco of Emmanuel College, the exhibition catalog, which was distributed to college and university libraries throughout Massachusetts, was made possible by contributions from the Massachusetts Cultural Council, Salem State College, Learning Society Incorporated, Tove Gerson, Martin Kilson, and Esther C. Williams. I wish to thank Sr. Frances Donahue of Emmanuel College for her assistance in administering the Massachusetts Cultural Council grant; Albert J. Hamilton, vice president of academic affairs at Salem State College, for his support of the catalog; and Patricia Zaido, director of Salem State College's Center for the Arts, for her promotion of the show.

The final phase in the creation of *Claiming Place* has been the writing of this ethnographic study of Biracial identity issues as perceived by Biracial young adults of diverse racial heritages. During the writing of this book, I have benefited from a sabbatical leave from my responsibilities as dean of the graduate school at Salem State College and from an appointment as research associate at the Peabody Museum of Harvard University. I wish to thank my colleagues Mary Jane Anderson, Margaret Bishop, and Elizabeth T. Kenney for assuming my responsibilities during my leave. I also am most appreciative of the critical reading that

Hannah Kilson-Kuchtic and Theresa Monaco gave to a preliminary draft of this manuscript and that George C. Bond and Charles Duncan gave to a later version. My revisions based on their comments and suggestions have enhanced this book—its limitations are, of course, my responsibility. I also thank Jane Garry and Lisa Webber for shepherding the manuscript through the publication process.

This book is dedicated to my husband and children, who have shared my journey and enriched my life in countless ways.

Part I

Biracial American Experience in the Post–Civil Rights Era

Biracial Americans

HISTORICAL AND CONTEMPORARY PERSPECTIVES

Throughout history, wherever and whenever peoples of different cultures and races have met they have exchanged ideas and genes. This interchange has been so extensive that today there are greater differences within "races" than between them. In fact, scientists recently determined that less than .012% genetic difference exists between the various strands of humanity (Hoffman 1994: 4). Despite the intermingling of Native Americans, Europeans, Africans, and Asians in North America for nearly four centuries, Americans have found acknowledging this reality problematic within the framework of Northern European hegemony. Over the past half century, this European American sociocultural ascendancy has been increasingly challenged by the courts and by people of color. In the Civil Rights era of the fifties and sixties and in subsequent decades, traditional social constructs regarding race relations disintegrated and new ones began to emerge. Attendant on these changes, various social trends evolved including a growing and increasingly visible cadre of mixed race Americans who now are claiming place in American society.

During the 1990s, public awareness of mixed race Americans has increased significantly. In mainstream newspapers and magazines, in col-

lege campus newspapers and quasi-popular racially targeted
publications, in scholarly journals and books, on television programs
and the internet, information relating to the experience of mixed race
Americans frequently appears. Some sources chronicle the significant
increase in interracial marriages and offspring since 1960, some describe the evolution of the grassroots movement successfully demand-
ing the inclusion of multiracial census category options in the year
2000, some emphasize race as a social construct rather than a biological
phenomenon, some comment on transracial adoption concerns, and
some discuss racial identity issues; others focus on existential aspects of
multiracial people's realities.[1] While there is increasing awareness of
multiracial Americans in the public consciousness, the complex diversity among multiracial Americans is less widely recognized.

Although interracial marriages increased by more than 800% between 1960 and 1990 so that today one in twenty-five couples is an interracial couple, American "races" are not intermarrying equally (Lind
1998:38). "The marriages of blacks to whites equaled 9 percent of all
intermarried couples in 1998, while the marriages of Asians to whites
equaled 19 percent, [Native Americans to whites 12%,] and Hispanics
to whites, 52 percent" (Phillip Martin 1999: D2). Since Hispanics,
Asians, and American Indians marry European Americans at much
higher rates than African Americans do, Michael Lind argues that the
United States of the twenty-first century will not have a non-White majority but a "white mixed-race majority" and a "black minority" (Lind
1998: 38–39).

Not only have the number of interracial marriages in American society increased dramatically over the past thirty years, but the socioeconomic attributes of interracial partners have changed. Whereas during
the first half of the twentieth century most marriages between African
Americans and European Americans were between individuals of lower
socioeconomic status, during the second half of the century, most interracial marriages have been between middle- and upper middle-class
people with respect to education and income (Williamson 1980:
188–189; Spickard 1989: 281, 308). Moreover, "what began to happen in America in the 1970s was . . . the growth of an opportunity for
individuals to resolve their personal identity dilemmas by embracing
both halves of their inheritance—not as half-breeds, but as people enti-
tled to identify fully with both" (Spickard 1989: 368). "The carriers of
this new blended identity are primarily . . . 'first generation' individuals.
. . . In the 1990s, a growing number of these individuals are challenging
the rule of hypodescent by 'unsevering' ties with their European Amer-

ican background and European Americans; they seek to do this without diminishing their affinity with the experience of African Americans. . . by affirming an integrative identity that has both the black and white communities as reference groups; or a pluralistic identity that blends aspects of the black and white communities but is neither" (Daniel 1996: 123). In this book I explore how some young adult Biracial Americans who grew up in the post-Civil Rights era perceive that they have managed race and identity issues over the course of their lives.

Before doing so, I want to comment briefly on several contemporary dilemmas associated with American racial classification systems, the most fundamental dilemma of which is, "What is race?" What do we mean by this concept that bedevils American social consciousness? Among social scientists today, "race" is regarded as a social construct rather than a physical reality (e.g., Smedley 1997: 52, 50). However, as Mukhopadhyay and Moses recently have observed, "[R]aces, though social constructions, do have a material reality and are in some sense and in some context biological groupings." (Mukhopadhyay and Moses 1997: 524). The most formal statement of the current version of the U.S. "folk taxonomy of categories of people" or "races" is found in the census categories.

Based on the Office of Management and Budget (OMB) Directive 15 of 1977, the 1990 census recognizes monoracial groupings and some ethnic differentiation.[2] Since the census categories do not include any multiracial options, mixed race individuals are classified in one or another of the monoracial categories. "Until a change in policy in 1989, biracial babies with a white parent were assigned the racial status of the nonwhite parent. Otherwise, multiracial babies of two parents of color . . . were assigned the race of the father. . . . [S]ince 1989, [a] new policy directs information keepers to designate *all* infants the same race as their mothers" (Root 1996: xviii–xix). In response to pressure from the multiethnic movement, the 2000 census will allow individuals to select as many racial labels as they "need" (Stanfield 1997).

Although the U.S. folk taxonomy of race may only now be beginning to recognize the social reality of multiracial Americans, multiracial Americans have always existed. Indeed, our census categories recognized a "mulatto" category between 1850 and 1920. For most of the twentieth century, however, multiracial Americans were enjoined to select a monoracial label. Moreover, in the United States the racial identification of a mixed race person has been governed by the principle of hypodescent, whereby the mixed race offspring assumes the racial identity of the lower-status group parent. Lewis Gordon argues that "The 'child' . . . of white-non-white liaisons exists as an onto-biological point of difference from at least one parent. One finds, in such circumstances, a rigid order of hierarchies according to social subordination. . . . Thus, in all matrices it is the white parent who loses onto-racial connections to her or his offspring" (Gordon 1997: 56). In his comparative study of mixed race rules around the world, F. James Davis found the hypodescent rule to be both unique to the United States (Davis 1991: 13) and distinctive in its application to Biracial Americans with an African American parent (Davis 1991: 12). Davis argues that today, "[T]hose persons in the United States who are partly descended from American Indians, Japanese Americans, Filipino Americans, or one of the other racially distinctive minorities besides blacks. . . represent . . . an assimilating minority, one that is being incorporated into the life of the dominant community" (Davis 1991: 117). While the structural position of multiracial Americans with African American parentage may differ from that of multiracial Americans with other heritages, "[c]ontemporary research and conceptualization on identity suggests parallels across different mixtures" (Root 1996: xx). In this book I, too, explore the extent to which multiracial Americans of different racial heritages share similar existential self-perceptions of otherness.

While I use the term "Biracial American" to refer to people whose parents belong to different socially recognized racial groups, I appreciate that the racial heritage of many Americans is infinitely more complex. Given the principle of hypodescent, most African Americans are of mixed race heritage. Given the assimilating principle associated with other American racial groups, many European Americans have Native American or Asian ancestry. Among the Biracial young adults who participated in my research, several alluded to more complex racial heritages for their parents of color. At least one African American parent had a European American grandmother, while other African American parents claimed Native American as well as African American heritages. Nevertheless, since all project participants identified their birth parents as belonging to different racial groups, I consider all of them to be "first generation" Biracial Americans.

Twentieth-century social science inquiry into mixed race people's realities begins with Edward Byron Reuter's *The Mulatto in the United States*. Published in 1918, this pioneering work reflects its time in its racism and classism but provides a valuable compendium of information about the growth and status attributes of the mulatto population, especially mulattoes' leadership role within African America after the

Civil War. Joel Williamson's *New People: Miscegenation and Mulattoes in the United States* (1980) carries the exploration of Reuter's concerns into the post–Civil Rights era with sensitivity to changing sociopolitical circumstances. Paul R. Spickard's *Mixed Blood: Intermarriage and Ethnic Identity in Twentieth Century America* (1989) addresses intermarriage comparatively over time and for different ethnic groups. Authored by multiracial scholars, the essays collected in Maria P.P. Root's *Racially Mixed People in America* (1992) and *The Multiracial Experience* (1996) analyze important demographic, classificatory, identity, developmental, and public policy topics from diverse disciplinary perspectives. Additional social science literature about mixed race issues in the nineties include Kathleen Korgen's *From Black to Biracial* (1998) and Charmaine L. Wijeyesinghe's "Understanding and Responding to the Racial Identity Development of Multiracial Students" (1994).

Most of the recent literature on Biracial Americans, however, is experiential and has appeared in trade books and popular media. Landmark television shows include June Cross' "*Secret Daughter*" (1996), "*A Question of Color*" (1994), "*Are You Black, White or Other?*" (1997), and "An American Love Story" (1999). In Lise Funderburg's *Black, White, Other: Biracial Americans Talk About Race and Identity* (1994), sixty-two African American/European American adults of varying ages reflect upon their life experiences. In Claudine Chiawei O'Hearn's *Half and Half: Writers on Growing Up Biracial and Bicultural* (1998), several authors explore their experiences as either Biracial Americans or the parents of multiracial children.

This book differs from previous books on Biracial American young adults in that it seeks to present an ethnographic overview of major issues in the lives of a diverse set of Biracial Americans of the post–Civil Rights generation as well as enable individual voices to be heard through responses to specific questions about their experiences as Biracial Americans. At the time that they were interviewed, these Biracial Americans ranged in age from mid-twenties to early thirties. Thus, they were adults with some experience of the world beyond their natal families. Moreover, they all belonged to the same generation of Biracial Americans.

Born on the crest of the Civil Rights Movement but coming of age in the United States at a time when Biraciality was less widely acknowledged than it is at the opening of a new century, the participants in this project represent a transitional generation of Biracial Americans. Only as young adults have most perceived that they had the option of publicly affirming all of their racial heritages. Many of the Biracial Americans who participated in this study perceive that their sociocultural experiences and expectations are different from younger Biracial Americans, who frequently articulate a blended racial identity for themselves.

SOME METHODOLOGICAL CONSIDERATIONS

This study of Biracial American racial identity is based on ethnographic interviews conducted in 1993–1994. As I developed plans for this study, I decided to interview fifty young adults, as I thought that this number would provide me with a large enough sample to establish patterns of commonality as well as differences in experiences and views. Ultimately I interviewed fifty-two young adult Biracial Americans over ten months between August 1993 and May 1994.

I used "snowball" sampling to find project participants. A few I knew before the study began; others were referred to me either by colleagues or by project participants. Not everyone whom I approached consented to be interviewed. Moreover, there were potential interviewees of whom I was aware but did not contact or could not reach before I had achieved my full complement of project participants.

I first approached potential project participants with a letter explaining the project and inviting their participation in it, as well as requesting that they complete a form about their personal and family backgrounds. A follow-up telephone call set an interview date either in person or by telephone. Twelve interviews were conducted in person in the Boston area; forty were conducted by telephone across the country from western Massachusetts through Virginia and Illinois to California and Washington. The ethnographic interviews were semistructured in that all participants were asked the same questions, but follow-up questions often differed. The interviews ranged from forty minutes to three hours in length, with most lasting one hour and a half. With participants' permission, all interviews were taped and later transcribed.

The interviews explored project participants' memories of racial identity issues as they were growing up and their current perspectives on race in their adult lives. Information derived from these interviews and from four focus groups conducted with several project participants constitutes the data for this study.

Given the sensitivity of my research inquiry, I consider the "snowball" method of finding project participants not only appropriate but probably essential. Nevertheless, I recognize that the method may have led to regional, socioeconomic, and racial bias in my interview sample.

Living in Massachusetts, my most immediate contacts are in the north-eastern United States. Project participants, however, readily referred me to Biracial American friends and siblings in the Midwest and the West. While there is clearly a bicoastal bias to my sample, in the United States today Biracial Americans live disproportionately on the West and East coasts. Although most of the project participants hold middle- and upper middle-class occupational positions, their socioeconomic status corresponds to that of their generation of Biracial Americans. Finally, while Biracial Americans in the United States today are more often Asian American/European American or Latino American/European American than African American/European American, my project participants are disproportionately African American/European American people. Nevertheless, I would argue for the experiential significance of the Biracial American whose heritage is partially African American in American society today, given the unique history and contemporary status of African Americans in the United States.

In this book, which seeks to understand the personal social constructs of multiracial Americans, I use two sets of "racial labels": personal labels and analytical labels. The personal racial labels are those that project participants use to identify themselves, such as "Black," "Korean," "German American," "Jewish," and "Biracial." Personal racial labels sometimes confound racial, religious, and ethnic categories. In this book, such personal labels appear in quotations from project participants' discourse.

The analytical labels, which specify the racial identity of project participants and their parents in either ethnographic analysis or citations, differentiate major racial groupings, including African American, Asian American, European American, Latino American, and Native American. Occasionally, these broad analytical categories are further differentiated to convey significant geocultural realities such as Middle Eastern, Afro-Caribbean, or Afro-Latino. Parents who were born outside the United States are designated in analytical labels only by their georacial origin, such as African, Asian, or European, though they may be identified in personal labels as Chinese, Dominican, or German. I have used the convention of having the father's racial identity precede that of the mother in Biracial labels. A person identified as European American/Asian, for example, has a European American father who was born in the United States and an Asian mother born in Asia. I have also chosen to use the label "Latino" rather than "Hispanic" to clarify the Caribbean or Latin American heritage of these individuals. Finally, I have chosen to capitalize racial labels both to denote their referential significance and to create consistency and equivalence among racial labels.

PROFILE OF PROJECT PARTICIPANTS

The young adult Biracial Americans with whom I talked shared the experience of being born in the 1960s. They were born at the time when Biracial American babies were automatically racially identified with their parent of color and with their father if both parents were people of color. As children of the sixties, these young adults matured in the United States during decades of increasing non-White immigration from Asia and Latin America and of expanding opportunities for the social and political participation of Americans of color.[3]

These first-generation Biracial Americans nevertheless differed in many ways—in their appearance, the composition of their natal families, the communities in which they grew up, their memories of family and racial issues, and their aspirations and expectations for the future. Although their parents include African Americans and European Americans, European Americans and Asian Americans, Asian Americans and African Americans, and European Americans and Latino Americans, their skin tones range from very light to very dark, their hair color and texture from blond and wavy to dark and very curly, their facial features from narrow to broad. Most grew up in households with their parents as only children or with their parents and siblings; if parents' marriages dissolved, many lived with their mothers; a few lived only with their mothers throughout their childhood, and some grew up in adoptive families. Like other American families, theirs had moved around. During their childhood, most had lived at some time in an urban neighborhood; many had resided in suburban communities and a few in rural ones. In addition, many had lived abroad; several were born overseas, coming to the United States as very young children; others had a year or two of international experience associated with their parents' careers. Although most had attended neighborhood public schools, others had studied in independent institutions. These young adult Biracial Americans' sociocultural diversity is matched by the variety of their racial experiences and their aspirations for the future.

At the time of my interviews with them, these young adults were living on the East Coast, on the West Coast, and in the Midwest.[4] They were in their late twenties and early thirties.[5] Most were single, a number were married with children of their own or partnered in a significant

Table I
Profile of Project Participants[1]

RESIDENCE		OCCUPATIONS	
Northeast:	19	Student:	11
Mid-Atlantic:	16	Job Seeker:	5
Midwest:	7	Service, Sales,	
West:	10	Clerical:	10
		Professional:	26

SEX			
Female:	33	**PERSONAL INCOME[2]**	
Male:	19	$10,000-$29,000:	14
		$30,000-$49,000:	14
AGE		$50,000-$99,000:	7
24-29 years:	30	$150,000:	1
30-34 years:	22		

		EDUCATION[3]	
MARITAL STATUS		High School:	1
Single:	32	Some college:[4]	10
Married:	19[5]	Baccalaureate:	25
Divorced:	1	Master's:[6]	10
		Doctorate:	6

1. This is a profile of project participants at the time of their interviews in 1993–94.
2. These personal income ranges pertain to the 36 non-students employed outside of the home.
3. Highest level of education completed.
4. Some college or technical college education.
5. Of those who are married, 14 have children; 5 are childless.
6. Master's degree or post-master's certificate.

relationship, and one was divorced. Among them were nine sets of siblings and four sets of spouses.

Since the youngest person interviewed was twenty-four years old, all had some experience of living independently of their parental homes and of the world of work. Their occupations ranged from undergraduate or graduate student through job seeker, and sales, service, or clerical positions to professional occupations. Of those who were employed outside the home, personal incomes ranged from $10,000 to more than $150,000. Their educational backgrounds were consistent with their occupational statuses; at the time of the interviews, six held doctorates, ten a master's degree or post–master's certificate, twenty-six a baccalaureate degree, six had had some college or technical college experience, and the remainder had completed high school. Thus, the project participants were well-educated young adults with middle- or upper middle-class occupational aspirations and achievements.

Drawing upon the memories and perceptions of these Biracial Americans, I discuss issues relating to sociocultural realities associated with biraciality in the chapters that follow. Chapter 2 explores family and race with reference to both the families in which people grew up and the families that they have established or hope to establish. Chapter 3 probes racial identity issues during participants' lives, comparing siblings and spouses wherever possible. Chapter 4 examines racial realities in adult lives, analyzing both evaluative perceptions of being Biracial in late twentieth-century America as well as life choices and race. Chapter 5, the final chapter in part I, illuminates recurrent systemic and personal themes in Biracial American life experiences. Part II demonstrates the diversity of perception and experience of the Biracial Americans participating in this project, for its chapters record responses to several interview questions. Finally, the epilogue highlights major findings of this study and presents a deconstruction of race in America today.

NOTES

1. See Bibliography. The list of topics includes: Biracial identity development, concept of race, interracial adoption, interracial dating, interracial marriage, mixed race demographics, movement for multicultural census category, multiracial classification, race relations, racial identity issues, and such experiential categories as autobiography, colorism, family perspectives, and parental perspectives on children.

2. The current racial/ethnic categories are American Indian or Alaska Native; Asian or Pacific Islander; Black, not of Hispanic origin; Hispanic; White, not of Hispanic origin. The inadequacy of current government racial classifications is critiqued effectively in Carlos A. Fernandez, "Government Classification of Multiracial/Multiethnic People," in Root (1996): 15–36 and Deborah A. Ramirez, "Multiracial Identity in a Color-Conscious World," in Root (1996): 49–62.

3. For an insightful analysis of major demographic trends with respect to American "minorities" since the 1960s, see Deborah A. Ramirez, "Multicultural Identity in a Color-Conscious World," in Root (1996): 49–62.

4. At the time of the interviews, 16 (31%) lived in Massachusetts, 3 in Connecticut, 16 in the Mid-Atlantic, 7 in the Midwest, and 10 in the West.

5. See Table I.

2

Biracial Americans and Their Families

Families find their realities in the memories of children now grown to adulthood and the aspirations that these young adults have for the future. While information about household composition and parental occupation have objective reality, the quality of remembered relationships within families is much more subjective, though equally, if not more, significant for understanding human life experiences. This chapter interweaves objective and subjective data as it addresses issues of familial relationships and race in childhood and young adulthood.

REMEMBERING CHILDHOOD FAMILIES AND RACE

The families in which project participants grew up varied demographically and structurally. Not only were parents' racial identities and socioeconomic statuses diverse, but their households differed in structure and modes of affiliation. These young adults variously recalled relationships with their parents and their siblings, as well as racial issues inside and outside the home.

These Biracial Americans identified their birth parents as Africans, African Americans, Asians, European Americans, Europeans, Latinos, Middle Easterners and Caribbean Islanders. Although most fathers are people of color and most mothers are European Americans, the diver-

sity of parents' racial backgrounds is greater than these facts suggest.
Among the birth fathers, thirty-four are Black (either African or African
American), fourteen are European American, three are Asian, and one
is African American and Native American.[1] Among the birth mothers,
twenty-eight are European American or European, ten are Asian, seven
are African Americans, five are mixed race women from the Caribbean
Islands, and two are African American and Native American.[2]

During their offsprings' childhood, most birth parents were married
to one another, many divorced, some never married, and three marriages dissolved through the father's death.[3] Of the eight birth parents
who never married, six of their children were adopted—three by African American couples, two by European American couples, and one by
a Biracial American couple; the other two continued to live with their
mothers. Of the three adopted by African American couples, two did
not know about their Biracial parentage until late adolescence.

In their early childhood, most project participants lived in households in which their birth or adoptive parents' marriage was the first for
both partners.[4] Although one-quarter of the childrearing parents had
only one offspring together, the majority had two to four children together. Moreover, fathers were more likely to have had children with

Table II
Racial Identity of Birth Parents

BIRTH PARENTS' RACIAL IDENTITY	PROJECT PARTICIPANTS' SEX	
BIRTH FATHER	**FEMALE**	**MALE**
Asian:	2	1
Black:[1]	23	11
Black/Native American:	1	-
European American:	7	7
BIRTH MOTHER		
African American:	1	6
Asian:	6	4
Black/Native American:	1	1
European American:	21	7
Mixed Race Caribbean:[2]	4	1

1. This category includes African and African American.
2. This category includes Afro-Caribbean and Latino-Caribbean women.

other wives than mothers with other husbands, for while eleven mothers had given birth to only one child, only four fathers had a single child.

Parental occupations were predominantly professional, with corresponding educational backgrounds.[5] African American, European American, and Asian American fathers were college professors; Asian fathers also included a carpenter and a chemist; European American fathers also included lawyers, librarians, a doctor, and an engineer; African American fathers included college deans, physicians, retired soldiers, a lawyer, a construction company owner, an actor, and a musician. Among African American and European American mothers were college professors and deans, teachers, school librarians, saleswomen, and foundation managers; among Asian and European American mothers were a few homemakers; among European American mothers were also social workers, artists, a personnel director, and a nurse; among Asian mothers were also a bilingual secretary and accountants; among African American mothers were also a writer, a daycare manager, and a substance abuse counselor. Complementing these occupations are parents' educational achievements. All fathers had completed high school and all but two mothers, who were born in Asia, had as well. Thirty-seven mothers and thirty-three fathers had graduated from college, while twenty-five fathers and nine mothers held doctorates.

While they were growing up, half of the project participants lived with both parents and their siblings; the other half lived at some time in

Table III
Parents' Educational and Occupational Profile[1]

FATHERS' EDUCATION		MOTHERS' EDUCATION	
Doctorate:	25	Doctorate:	9
Master's:[2]	7	Master's:	16
Baccalaureate:	1	Baccalaureate:	12
Some College:	5	High School:	13
High School:	14	Middle School:	2

FATHERS' OCCUPATION		MOTHERS' OCCUPATION	
Professional:	36	Professional:	31
Managerial:	6	Managerial:	2
Sales/Service:	9	Sales/Clerical:	6
Unknown:	1	Homemaker:	8
		Retired:	5

1. In this table, "Parent" means childhood caregiver, whether biological or adoptive. The educational achievement and occupations are those at the time of the interviews.
2. This category includes both master's degree and post-master's certificate.

a single parent household with their mothers. Ten parents' marriages ended through death or divorce before project participants were twelve years old; four experienced such losses during adolescence. When divorce or death destroyed parents' marriages, the children continued to live with their mothers, their mothers and their siblings, or occasionally with their mothers and their maternal grandparents. A few subsequently lived with their mothers' new spouses, and one alternated between her mother's household and her father's after her parents' divorce. Some individuals had more complex residential histories: one woman initially lived with her birth mother, then with adoptive parents until their divorce; thereafter, she lived with her adoptive mother until she went to college; another woman lived with her mother and her mother's boyfriends and spouses as well as her European American half-siblings; yet another woman lived with her mother and half siblings until being reared by a foster mother with whose children she shared a home. Of the eleven men and fifteen women who lived in a single-parent household during childhood, thirteen were reared by European American mothers, ten by African American or mixed race mothers, and three by Asian mothers. Among these young adults who lived in single-parent households growing up, ten had no contact with their fathers during those years and only three felt emotionally close to their absent fathers.

Recalling Relationships with Parents

Living with parents does not necessarily mean that children remember feeling emotionally close to them. Among the twenty-eight who grew up with both parents, eighteen felt close to both parents, three to their mothers, and one to her father, while four did not feel close to either parent. Among the twenty-four living with their mothers during all or most of their growing-up years, sixteen felt close to their mothers and eight felt distant from them.

These young adults had diverse memories of emotional closeness or distance from their parents. In general, project participants felt closer to their mothers than their fathers: thirty-seven said that they felt close to their mothers, while twenty said that they felt close to their fathers. Most of those who felt close to their fathers said that they felt close to both parents. These were parents living together with their children; only two of these children said that they felt close to their fathers but not their mothers.[6] In general, coresidence and emotional closeness are correlated among these young adult Biracial Americans.

Table IV
Project Participants' Relationship to Parents During Growing-up
Years

RELATIONSHIP	MOTHER/FATHER HOUSEHOLD	MOTHER-HEADED HOUSEHOLD
Close To Mother And Father	18	1
Close To Mother	3	15
Close To Father	1	1
Not Close To Mother And Father	6	7

The remembered sources of closeness to and distance from parents are various. Among those who felt close to their parents were an African American/European American woman adopted by a European American couple who recalled, "My parents raised us to celebrate our individuality—I have a brother and sister that are their natural children—they really raised us to celebrate our individuality; . . . it was a very good, very solid relationship" (Voice 17). Another African American/European American woman said, "I think that my relationship with my parents was really positive. . . . I see my mother as much more primary—responsible for who I am and what I have become as a person. Though my father . . . I really took from [him] my incredible loyalty to my family—almost loyalty to a fault. I think that I developed that from him and I also obviously developed from him a kind of very strong sense of being proud about being a Black person, but I also got that from my mother" (Voice 41). Others, however, had less positive remembrances of their relationships with their parents. One European American/African American woman remembered, "It was a difficult relationship, because my father's theory on raising children was different than my mother's theory. . . . My father's theory was talking and my mother's was discipline. . . so very conflicting" (Voice 11). An African American/Asian man recalled, "Since there were so many of us, I guess they didn't spend so much time with each one of us. . . . We just did our own thing—I did, anyway" (Voice 47). A woman of Asian and European American parentage remembered her relationship with her parents as "tension-filled at almost all times. My dad is just a hard person to get along with in general, although I'm the child that everyone thinks resembles him. . . . Then my sister was . . . the lighter child who resembled Mom and they were really close." (Voice 36) Finally, a young man of African American and European American parentage said, "It wasn't a great [relationship] when I was younger, just because they're so academically oriented and I wasn't academically oriented at all. My dad was the disciplinarian, so I was sort of scared of him." (Voice 48) As these project participants' statements indicate, sources of remembered closeness and distance in relationships with parents include parental affirmation of and involvement in children's lives, compatibility of parents' and children's personalities and interests, perceived differences in parental childrearing orientations, or preferences for different children.[7]

A consideration of emotional closeness to parents and racial identity discloses some noteworthy differentiations. Among the ten Biracial young adults whose parents were both people of color, eight (80%) recalled feeling close to their mothers growing up and four (40%) felt closer to their fathers. Among twenty-seven people with European American mothers, twenty-one (75%) felt close to their mothers, whereas 16 (67%) of the twenty-four with mothers of color felt close to them. Of the thirty-eight people with fathers of color, 17 (45%) felt close to them, but only 3 (21%) of the 14 with European American fathers felt close to their fathers. Consistent with the correlation of coresidence and remembrance of feeling close to parents, most project participants remembered a close relationship with their mothers irrespective of race during childhood.

With respect to fathers, however, some notable differences exist when coresidence and race are considered.[8] During their children's growing-up years, a larger proportion of fathers of color lived with their wives and children than European American fathers (61% fathers of color; 43% European American fathers). A significantly larger proportion of fathers of color who were coresident with their children had close relationships with them than did coresident European American fathers (69% fathers of color; 33% European American fathers). Thus, not only were European American fathers more likely not to live with their children during their growing-up years than fathers of color, but they were more likely to have distant relationships with their children whether or not they lived together. These differences suggest that while men in American society tend to be less involved in their children's lives than women, European American men are less prepared for and less capable of coping with the complexities of Biracial family life; consequently, they are more likely to be distant from their Biracial children. Men of color, on the other hand, have lifelong experience of dealing with American racist patterns; color, therefore, is a source of affinity

Table V
Project Participants' Relationships with Fathers of Color and
European American Fathers

| | RELATIONSHIP WITH FATHER | |
	CLOSE	DISTANT
FATHERS OF COLOR		
Mother/Father Household	16	7
Mother-Headed Household	1	14
EUROPEAN AMERICAN FATHERS		
Mother/Father Household	2	4
Mother-Headed Household	1	7

rather than a potential source of distance between them and their Biracial children.

Children may perceive changes in their relationships with their parents over the years. One young European American/African American woman perceptively recounted her evolving relationship to her parents, with both of whom she now feels close. "I think for a while after the divorce, I was really distant from my father . . . and I was very, very close to my mother; then . . . much later, when I was in college, my father and I became really, really close again. And I became a little bit estranged from my mother, but at this point, I'm close to both of them, very close to both of them—they're like my friends as opposed to my parents" (Voice 43). The divorce of parents of a European American/Afro-Caribbean woman led to significant changes in her relationships with them. She stated, "I remember being very attached to my dad. . . . I was so attached to him that when they decided to divorce, he was the one who had to tell me, because I would not have taken it well from my mother. . . . So it was very important that I maintain contact with him. . . . But somewhere along the line . . . I did become very attached to my mother . . . and then I became very rejecting of my father" (Voice 37). As these statements suggest, people may feel more distant from a beloved parent as they grow older or closer to one to whom they previously felt less close. Situational and developmental factors contribute to children's views of their changing relationships with parents.

   Nevertheless, emotional closeness with parents does not imply that
children remember sharing feelings about race with them as they were
growing up. Twenty-two (44%) project participants said that they did
not remember sharing their feelings about race with anyone growing
up; among these twenty-two are sixteen who said that they felt close to
one or both parents. Of the eleven who said that they felt distant from
both parents, five said that they shared their feelings about race with
family members or friends. Biracial women were less likely to remember
sharing their feelings about race with anyone than were Biracial men.[9]
In describing her experiences of racism in school as a young child, an
African American/ European American woman summarized her experience and that of others: "I've talked to a lot of other mixed race kids
who say that they never brought this stuff home with them. It was
something that you just didn't bring home with you. I never brought it
home; I never mentioned it." (Voice 16)
   Most project participants have siblings, for merely eleven are only
children, and they occupy various birth-order positions within their sibling groups. Many have younger siblings or older siblings, while several
are middle children with both older and younger siblings.[10] Moreover,
twenty of the fifty-two interviewees had at least one sibling who also
participated in the project. Among the nine sibling sets of project participants, some individuals differed in their perceptions of their relationships with their parents during their growing-up years. Although
siblings in five sets claimed similar relationships with their parents, siblings in four sets did not. The siblings who had similar views all lived
with both parents throughout their growing-up years. Three sets of siblings felt close to both parents while they were young, another set felt
close to their mother but not their father, and the other felt distant from
both parents. Two sisters both felt distant from their mother during
their childhood, but one felt close to her father despite her parents' divorce while the other did not. One brother and his sister felt close to
both their parents, while another brother did not feel close to either
parent. These siblings lived with both parents throughout their growing-up years, as did a pair of siblings in which one woman felt close to
both her father and mother, while her brother only felt close to their
mother. Finally, two brothers felt distant from their absent father, but
only one felt close to their mother, with whom they lived as they were
growing up. Thus, living in the same house with both parents may, but
need not, lead siblings to have similar views of their relationships with
their parents.

Irrespective of their remembered relationships with their parents, many individuals recalled both positive and negative aspects of their Biracial growing up. Since many of the experiences leading to these assessments occurred outside the family context, they will be discussed later. Here I wish to note how parents' cultural naïveté variously contributed to their offsprings' childhood experiences as Biracial Americans. Some participants considered that their immigrant parents' lack of understanding about American race relations increased the difficulties that they experienced in dealing with racial issues as children, while others thought that it made racial matters less potent for them. For example, one African American/ European man said, "Another reason why [my mom] couldn't deal [was] because she was an immigrant herself and she had to get used to what was going on here in the United States and she was White. Maybe if she was Black and had come from Africa and had experienced racism . . . she would have brought me up a little differently" (Voice 20).

While cultural naïveté can be problematic, it can also be perceived as beneficial. One African American/European American woman thought her mother's lack of concern about certain African American cultural prejudices had had a positive effect on her racial identity development. She remarked, "I think one of the things that struck me, when I saw ["A Question of Color," a television program on intraracial prejudice] for the first time was how I didn't grow up with that kind of baggage. There were a lot of issues [in the program] around 'good hair,' 'bad hair,' and around issues of skin tone and being better because you were lighter skinned. And that just wasn't part of the dialogue or part of the experience. . . . It wasn't an issue for me, but as I interacted more with people of different races and more African Americans it really came into the conversation" (Voice 41). Parental cultural naïveté, therefore, can contribute negatively and positively to their Biracial children's development. (See chapter 8 for additional information about relationships with parents.)

Comparing Siblings' Racial Experiences

Although forty-one project participants have siblings, several siblings are not children of the same parents. Two Biracial young adults have half-siblings who are European Americans, and four discussed the experiences of their adoptive siblings who include Biracial Americans, African Americans, and European Americans. When asked to reflect upon how their racial experiences differed from that of their siblings while they were growing up, five (12%) said that they did not know, because they had never discussed their racial experiences with their brothers and sisters. Only three (7%) perceived their racial experiences to have been similar to their siblings' experiences.

Among Biracial siblings who have the same birth parents, many attributed different racial experiences to physical differences as well as to sociocultural and psychosocial factors. For example, one woman of African American and European American parentage stated, "My brother looks White and so his experience was totally the opposite of mine. . . . He would go to a job [in high school], and they'd find out that my father was Black and then they wouldn't talk to him, which was totally the opposite of me, because people were more interested in what my mother looked like than what my father looked like. And I also think that I identified more with being Black than my brother did" (Voice 13). Conversely, a European American/African American man asserted, "My sister had more Black friends than I did. . . . I think that's just because her skin tone is darker, she's more accepted by Black people. . . . I'm lighter than she is" (Voice 10). These and other Biracial Americans mentioned both skin tone and hair texture variations as physical factors accounting for differences in their and their siblings' racial experiences. Skin tone differences were noted by fourteen Biracial Americans as the principal reason behind siblings' different racial experiences. Darker siblings were often perceived as mingling more easily with African Americans and also as identifying more with Blacks and experiencing more racist encounters, while lighter skinned siblings were sometimes perceived as resisting being Black or, conversely, identifying themselves more strongly as Black than their darker siblings.

Among the sociocultural differences that nine project participants thought led to variant racial experiences for them and their siblings were: living in different residential neighborhoods, attending different schools, and establishing different friendship patterns. For example, one African American/European American woman had been bused to a predominantly White suburb for her schooling, whereas her brother attended a school in their urban neighborhood. Another, who had spent her earliest childhood years in Germany, considered that her brother, who grew up only in the United States, had developed a stronger African American identity than she. The psychosocial differences include different world views, differences in self-esteem, and developmental differences. An African American/Asian woman considered that her siblings had much more racialized world views than she, which she attributed to differences in personality, whereas an African American/European American man thought that his younger brother—who had spent all his life in a European American environment—knew nothing about African American life and culture. One African American/European American woman perceived that she and her two siblings struggled with racial identity issues at very different times in their lives. She said, "I think our experience of race—in the sense of the issue of [racial] identity—hit us at different points. I think mine was very early adolescence; I would say my sister's was much more high school . . . I think [for] my brother it is mid-twenties. I think [the racial identity issue] hit us at different points. . . . I think for me it was really the issue of being in progressively larger settings with other Blacks . . . in junior high school and it happened for my sister in high school" (Voice 29).

Finally, some attributed differences in racial experiences to birth order. A couple of project participants considered the eldest sibling a pace-setter who cushioned the negative impact of biraciality for younger siblings. One African American/European American man, for example, stated,

I should say that my [younger] brother has had it a lot easier than I have. . . . I'm no superhero, but I had confronted race issues when I moved to North Town that he never had to, because everybody already know who he was. . . . 'That's little Joe,' they would always say. . . . He's going to end up working in North Town, probably live his whole life there, and . . . he's happy with that. But that's something we have that differs, because I was the first son. And by the time he first came to school, I was already in third or fourth grade and I had been battling since first grade with all these kids. And they all knew who he was, because they knew who Joe was, and he never had that clash [about] . . . his race. (Voice 35)

Similarly, an African American/European American woman said,

I think that Sarah did have the experience of paving the way. . . . Nobody ever called me "nigger" and nobody ever called me "popcorn head." She experienced those things and I didn't. In some respects, I think that it's because she did that I didn't; other things came up [for me] but they were not nearly as blatant, and I was also always a lot more aggressive person. . . . When I was a kid, you bother me, get out of my way; I would warn you once and then if you did it again, I would drop you. (Voice 41)

The two project participants who have half siblings that are European American both asserted that growing up their siblings did not have to think about race as they did. They both perceived their birth parents'

European American children as "insulated from race." One Biracial
woman said, "[My White half-siblings] are very fortunate in that they
don't have to think about race. Their experience has differed in that I
don't think that they've ever experienced discrimination and I don't
think that they can imagine being told that they're not attractive—because they're not Black and because they're not White—the way that I
was told. . . . And I don't think that they feel an affinity with other people, because of their race" (Voice 43). Thus, this woman and the other
Biracial woman considered that their European American half siblings
enjoyed the advantages of "White-skin privilege."

Adoptive siblings discussed many of the same issues. One Biracial
American man who has an adoptive African American sister and adop-
tive European American siblings noted that his European American
siblings were very understanding of racial issues, while his African
American sister had more difficulty than he in accepting their European
American adoptive parents. A Biracial American woman adopted by a
European American couple said that when growing up, her European
American siblings neither had to endure the racial slurs that she did nor
could they understand her need for acceptance by others. Another Biracial American woman who was adopted by an African American couple
said that her adoptive Biracial American sister had more difficulty than
she in accepting her Biraciality, whereas she had searched for and found
her European American birth mother with the support of her African
American adoptive parents.

Relationships Outside the Home and Racial Issues

Among the many factors contributing to racial experiences and
memories are residential communities and schools, which provide important contexts for social interaction beyond the household in childhood. Although all the Biracial Americans whom I interviewed spent
their formative years in the United States, several were born outside the
United States in Asia, Europe, and the Caribbean. As children, many
also had some overseas experiences in Europe, Africa, Asia, Israel, and
the Caribbean.[11] Their American childhoods were spent on the East
Coast (61%), the Midwest (29%), and the West (10%).

Growing up, project participants lived in various kinds of communities. Many (29, or 56%) recalled initially living in an urban community,
others in a suburban community, a few in overseas communities. and one
in a rural community. Some moved from their first remembered homes
to urban communities in the United States, to suburban communities,

Table VI
Residential Communities During Growing-up Years

UNITED STATES[1]

Rural:	1
Suburban:	9
Suburban/Rural/Urban:	1
Suburban/Urban:	1
Urban:	17
Urban/Rural:	4
Urban/Suburban:	5
Urban/Rural/Urban/Suburban:	1

UNITED STATES AND OVERSEAS

Urban USA/Suburban Africa/	
Suburban USA:	2
Overseas/Urban USA:	3
Overseas/Rural USA:	1
Overseas/Suburban USA:	4
Suburban USA/Urban Africa	
Suburban USA:	3

1. The sequence of residential communities is reflected in their ordering. Thus, Suburban/Rural/Urban category means that during childhood, the individual lived first in a suburban community, then in a rural one, and later in an urban one.

and to rural communities. Although all of the rural communities were predominantly European American, some suburban communities were racially mixed, some urban communities were racially and socioeconomically mixed, and some were monoracial middle class urban communities of African Americans or European Americans.[12]

With respect to schooling, although half of the project participants attended public schools that mirrored their residential neighborhoods, the other half attended private or parochial schools for at least part of their schooling. While one person always attended private schools and five always went to parochial schools, most moved between different types of schools during their youth. Fifteen initially attended public schools before going to private schools; four attended private schools before attending public schools; and two began their schooling in parochial schools before going on to public schools. A number of people moved back and forth between public and independent schools throughout their school years. Some public and private schools were monoracial, whereas others were racially mixed. Thus, opportunities for friendships and encounters with diverse populations characterized most project participants' school days.

Looking back to childhood and adolescence, these young adults recall positive and negative aspects of their Biracial experience. Several discussed the special pride that they felt in being a bridge between different racial groups and valued their ability to move comfortably between different cultural worlds. Others mentioned the value of a dual heritage, a few noted their White-skin privilege, and several expressed delight in shattering racial stereotypes. Among the childhood liabilities that these Biracial young adults recalled, many centered on the impact of appearance issues associated with skin tone; the sense of not belonging to the culturally dominant group in their community—of not being African American in an African American neighborhood, of not being Latino in a Latino neighborhood, of not being European American in a European American neighborhood; the experience of peer rejection because of race; and the sense of not looking like their peers. A few mentioned being embarrassed by their biraciality, by their parent of color, or by their European American parent. Others avoided thinking about their biraciality or did not pursue their cultural heritages. One mentioned distress at his awareness that he behaved differently with European American and with African American peers.

The challenges and variant ways that individuals confronted dilemmas associated with biraciality are conveyed through the following statements. One African American/European American woman said, "In terms of being privileged—well, I was always in honors classes, so there was this kind of double status of being Black but being smart, which I'm sure was ascribed to being half White. So there was that aspect. You know, I can remember people saying things to me growing up, like teachers saying, 'You're the perfect color—you're just a little suntanned'" (Voice 1). A man of African American/Middle Eastern parentage recalled, "I remember back in first grade . . . [on] Parents' Day; my mom and dad would come to school at different times, because they had to work around their work schedules. And I remember that I wasn't proud, because I . . . had different colored parents. . . . And later on, I had shame for that" (Voice 4). Contrasting with this man's early childhood response to others' expectation of racial identity is the adolescent defiance of an African American/European American woman.

My memories are of flaunting in people's faces their own expectations of who they thought I was. . . ."So, your mom's here?" "Yeah." "Where is she?

Where?" And my mother'd be standing in a place where she could only be the person I was pointing at. I'd . . . describ[e] her to a tee, except I wouldn't describe her race, the color of her skin, purposely. There was no way people could know that it was other than she, except that they expected her to be a Black person, so they couldn't see her. (Voice 41)

A European American/Afro-Caribbean man recounted his boyhood outsider status in Miami. "Earlier in my life, particularly . . . in Miami when language was an issue, it was ethnicity and language access that seemed more of a liability than anything else. . . . In Miami, between . . . [the ages of eight and seventeen years], being whatever I was, not being Latino was a big deal in all kinds of ways—fitting into peer groups, getting dates, figuring out when people were having a joke at my expense" (Voice 15). The importance of such experiences outside the home for racial identity formation will be explored further in the next chapter, which deals with various aspects of Biracial identity.

RECALLING RELATIONSHIPS WITH PARENTS' RELATIVES

When asked about their relationships with their parents' families while growing up, most participants (37, or 71%) said that they had had close relationships with members of their mother's family, their father's family, or both parents' families.[13] Twenty-seven said that they were close to their mother's family members and sixteen to their father's family members. Of these, twelve were close to their mother's family members who were people of color and fifteen close to their mother's family members who were European Americans, whereas twelve were close to father's family members who were people of color and four to their European American father's family members. Twenty-four, therefore, were close to parental families of color and nineteen close to European American parental families. Almost two-thirds of those who said that they were close to one or both parental families were close to maternal family members, and a majority (56%) were close to a grandparental family of color.

One African American/European American woman described her perception of how she became close to both her parents' relatives and the significance of that experience for her.

I think that my parents really emphasized the importance of family in every way . . . and so we grew up spending a lot of time with aunts and uncles on both sides of the family. We spent a lot of time shuttling between Philadelphia and Boston, because it was very clear that it was important to my father that we knew his family and [some of his family] spent the summers with us. . . . It has created a very strong foundation in realizing the importance of having family and having people who are there to support you and the importance of knowing who those people are. Knowing your background and where you are from, I think helps you with the issue of identity. (Voice 29)

For this woman, then, close relationships with relatives helped her to deal with her biraciality.

Nevertheless, sixteen—or nearly one third—of the project participants said that they had no relationship with their father's family or mother's family, while one participant said that he was not close to either grandparental family. Among those who claim not to have had a relationship with members of their parents' natal families are individuals with African American, European American, and Asian grandparents. At the other end of the social continuum are those who lived with grandparental family members—one lived with her father's childless sister until she was seven, four lived with their European American maternal families and two lived with African American maternal families. (See chapter 8 for additional information about relationships with parents' families.)

One European American/African American man described the importance of his maternal grandparents in his boyhood. He said, "We lived with my grandparents until I was seven and I would say that my grandfather was in some ways my father; he did the disciplining. They actually did a lot of childcare, because my mom was away. . . . It was nice to have someone like my grandfather around in my early years, because he was a very wonderful man . . . whom everyone in the family adored for his honesty and integrity—just a hard working man" (Voice 38). Since this man's parents had divorced when he was very young, his African American grandfather became an important male role model for him.

Although young adult Biracial Americans attribute differences in the nature and quality of their relationships with grandparents, parents' siblings, and their families to various situational factors, three frequently mentioned circumstances were their parents' families' objections to their parents' Biracial marriage or relationship, geographical distance, and racial rejection. Eleven young adults mentioned familial objections to their parents' marriages. Objections to a child marrying an African American came from nine European American and two Asian families; one African American family was said to disapprove of their son marrying a European American woman. While in many instances these concerns abated with the passage of time and the birth of grandchildren, for several sets of grandparents these feelings impeded the development of close ties with Biracial grandchildren, nieces, and nephews.

One European American/African American woman conveyed the ambiguous complexity of relationships with grandparents and parents' siblings. She said,

When my parents married, my father's mother disowned him for marrying my mother, because she was Black. So early on my grandmother was very distant, but once I was born, she came onto the scene and took care of me a lot of the time. And I would go down South and spend a lot of time with my mother's family. . . . And I've always been close to my father's brother and his wife, though at different times I feel that I've had to check out of the White side of the family, . . . [because] there were certain things that I didn't feel that they could understand or . . . certain ways that they couldn't affirm me and my existence, and I felt sometimes being with them was very dangerous, because they would say things like, "You really have to do something with your hair"; or just little things like my grandmother saying, "You should change your clothes." I was always not right in some way, so I sort of steered clear of them until I was strong enough to be able to go back into that and say, "Well, I am who I am and that's that." (Voice 43)

Although this woman enjoyed good relationships with her parents' families, she clearly felt more comfortable with her African American relatives than with her European American ones, whose criticism made her feel insecure for many years.

A second factor affecting how often Biracial children interacted with their parents' families is geographical propinquity. More than one third of the interviewees (19, or 37%) said that they did not see their parents' families often, if at all, because they lived too far away. Quite a number of Asian grandparents lived in Japan and Korea, several European grandparents lived in Germany and England, while a few Black grandparents lived in the Caribbean and Nigeria. Nevertheless, living nearby does not guarantee that people will have close relationships with relatives. One young woman, for example, commented that although her paternal family had lived in the same neighborhood, she was never close to them.

Experiences of racial rejection also led to a lack of closeness between grandparental families and their Biracial grandchildren. One young woman told of her European American grandmother's explicit wish not to be identified as her grandmother; another recounted how her grandmother instructed her not to reveal her biraciality to the grandmother's friends. One young woman described how her existence was kept secret from several of her mother's European American relatives; she said, "My mother's parents I love very dearly, even though I don't really like that they kept me secret from my grandfather's mother. They've always treated me wonderfully and I have good rapport with my grandmother. . . . She was always very good to me, but my race was not acknowledged [by my grandparents]" (Voice 24). This woman's European American grandparents' failure to affirm her identity as a person of color diminished an otherwise loving relationship. Painful personal experiences of racial rejection do not engender strong, open relationships between grandparent and grandchild or aunt and niece.

Among these Biracial American young adults, most people were close to their maternal grandparents and nearly one third to their paternal grandparents, irrespective of race. Nevertheless, a majority of young adults were close to grandparents of color. These facts reflect both the matrilateral tendencies in American families and the greater acceptance by people of color for multiracial people in American society.[14]

CREATING FAMILIES AND IMAGINING THE FUTURE

As young adults, the Biracial Americans whom I interviewed have reflected upon their own formative familial years and considered the families that they wish to create for themselves. Some have already chosen marriage partners and begun to raise their own children. In establishing their families, they have drawn upon their past experiences as well as their aspirations for the future.

Like many other Biracial Americans, the project participants and their siblings are cosmopolitan in their choice of marriage partners.[15] Of the nineteen who are married or partnered, six are married to a Biracial person, five to a European American, one to a European, four to an African American or Black person, and three to a Latino American. Of the nineteen, twelve (63%) are women. Of the six married to European Americans or a European, five are women; of the three married to Latino Americans, all are men of African American/Asian parentage; of the four married to Blacks, all are women; of the six married to another Biracial person, two African American/European American women are married to African American/Asian American men, while three men and one woman have African American/European American

Table VII
Racial Identity of Spouses

PROJECT PARTICI- PANTS	SPOUSE'S RACIAL IDENTITY				
	BIRACIAL AMERICAN BLACK/ WHITE	BLACK/ ASIAN	LATINO AMERICAN	BLACK	WHITE
MEN					
BLACK/ASIAN	2	-	3	-	-
BLACK/WHITE	1	-	-	-	-
WHITE/BLACK	-	-	-	-	1
WOMEN					
BLACK/ASIAN	-	-	-	1	1
BLACK/WHITE	1	2	-	2	3
WHITE/ASIAN	-	-	-	-	1
WHITE/BLACK	-	-	-	1	-

Note: Black refers to people of African or African American descent; White refers to people of European or European American descent.

spouses.[16] The cosmopolitanism of project participants in their choice of spouses is further reflected in the diverse racial identities of siblings' spouses within the sibling groups interviewed: one African American/European American woman is married to a European, her sister to a man of Jamaican descent; one African American/Asian American man is married to a Latino American woman, whereas his brother is married to an African American/European American woman; one African American/European American woman is single; her sister is married to a European American man.

In addition to the siblings interviewed, project participants have sixteen more siblings who are married. Of these, eight who are African American/European Americans or Asian American/African Americans are married to African Americans, six who are also European American/African Americans and African American/Asian Americans have European American spouses, one sibling is married to a Native American, and one to a Biracial American. Thus, in choosing marriage partners, young adult Biracial Americans are continuing the cosmopolitanism of their parents' generation.

Irrespective of racial identity, project participants have chosen spouses of similar educational and occupational attainments. Almost three-quarters of the spouses have had some postsecondary schooling and six have completed master's or doctoral degrees. Thirteen have professional occupations such as research scientist, financial analyst, ar-

Table VIII
Spouses' Education and Occupation

	HUSBANDS' EDUCATION	WIVES' EDUCATION
High School	1	3
Some College	2	1
Baccalaureate	4	1
Master's	3	1
Doctorate	1	1
Unknown	1	

	HUSBANDS' OCCUPATION	WIVES' OCCUPATION
Professional	10	3
Sales/Service/Trade	2	2
Homemaker	--	2

chitect, and teacher, while the remainder are engaged in sales, service, trade, and homemaking fields.[17]

Of the project participants who are married, fourteen already have children whose well-being influences their choices of residential communities. Some value a diverse community for their children over other considerations; others prefer a middle-class neighborhood with good schools. Thus, for some Biracial parents racial identity issues assume greater salience than educational ones.

These divergent perceptions are reflected in the statements of three Biracial young adults. One man of African American/Asian parentage stated, "When we first moved out here, I didn't really care where I lived. Well, I wanted to live some place upper middle-class just so when my kids go to school, they'd learn" (Voice 26). In contrast, an African American/Asian woman said, "I prefer to be in a racially mixed area; I'm more comfortable in an area that's racially mixed or even predominantly Black, but it just so happens that over the last eight years, I've lived in predominantly White neighborhoods. . . . It's mostly had to do with my daughter's education; I've wanted her to have the best in education, so when they started having racial problems at her school out in Westwood, [we moved here]" (Voice 5). The singular importance of residential diversity, however, was voiced by another African American/Asian man. "We live in a suburb outside Eastside that is mixed—there are Black families, a lot of Asian families, and White. . . . I wanted to be in an area where my kids could identify with who they were instead of having to go through things that I did. It took me a lot of years. So I do not want to have my kids spend as much time as I did deciding who they are" (Voice 8). These three viewpoints indicate the range of perspectives on the relative importance of community diversity and educational quality.

Some young adults who are not yet married or who do not yet have children are concerned about their future children's racial identity and how race may affect their relationships. One young woman who is married to a European expressed concern that her children might feel less connection to her because she would be darker than they. Another does not wish to marry a European American, because she does not want her children to be embarrassed by her dark skin tone. Yet another who is European American/Afro-Latino wants to marry a Latino man so that her children will be recognized as Latino. Similarly, a young European American/African American man wishes to marry an African American woman in part to enjoy the warm values that he associates with African American culture. Thus, as these young adult Biracial Americans imagine their futures, they wish to protect their children and themselves from some of the race-related difficulties that they have encountered as children and as adults.

Young adult Biracial Americans convey these views in the following statements. A woman of Afro-Caribbean and European parentage related her friend's experience. "A friend . . . is very light skinned and her mother came for a track meet. One of the girls on the track team said, 'Oh, how nice of you to bring your maid with you to the track meet.' I would die if I had a child with a White man and that happened to me. . . . I don't want to have White children . . . I don't want to have . . . my kid be embarrassed with me" (Voice 28). A woman of African American and European American parentage gave a cultural rationale for choosing to have a Black family in the future.

I have decided that I am not going to have Biracial children . . . It was confusing [to be a Biracial child] . . . it was sometimes real painful, and I didn't think that there was a very strong support for it. To me the most important thing in human relations is support—emotional, intellectual, all kinds. . . . It seems natural to me that I would have a Black family, because I never had one, because I was adopted. . . . Also, I feel that Black culture needs me as much as I need it; I think that White culture is doing just fine. (Voice 17)

Another woman of European American and Afro-Latino parentage indicated why she wanted to marry a Latino. She said, "I've started to feel really strongly about who I marry. I'd like to marry a Hispanic man, because I don't want my kids to be Biracial; I think it's too hard. If I marry a Hispanic man, at least they're three-quarters something. I feel pretty strongly about that. I'd really like not to marry a man of a different race. . . . I think it's very, very hard growing up being half and half" (Voice 3). Another African American/European American woman worried about her connection with light-skinned children. She stated,

If my kids are really light skinned and they look like their dad, they'll be seen as White and they may have experiences that I'll have no way to connect to; that's another piece that's hard to think about as a parent. And I'm sure that my mother must have had to go through this—we, my sister and brother and I, have had experiences she will never know, she will never know what they meant or felt to us, or how we've endured them, or how it means to live our lives as African-Americans, because she is not. (Voice 41)

As young adults envisage their future parenting roles, they often draw lessons from their own pasts about how to address racial issues. Several stressed not only the importance of being open and forthright about racial issues but the significance of being visibly present for their children. One African American/European American man, for example, stated, "Relating to my own experience, . . . because my race is not apparent to people, one of the critical things in my life was my dad not being present in my experiences in high school and things like that. . . . My dad barely ever came to soccer games but whenever he did it was a big issue for me. . . . But I think the point of having it known absolutely without any question to everybody who needs to know it would be something that I would make a point about" (Voice 14). A European American/Afro-Latino woman stressed a variant on this theme. "One of my issues with my father is that to this day he doesn't really address the race issue. I'm just his daughter; my sister and I are his daughters. So what [that] we call ourselves 'Latinas..' . . . He just never put himself in our place. So I know that . . . I would deal with the race issue. . . . I think you have to do that work at home" (Voice 37).

As Biracial Americans talked about their childhood experiences in families and their hopes and concerns for their children in families, the commonality and diversity of their experiences are striking. The life-long impact of negative racial encounters in childhood, on the one hand, and the ability to transcend racial boundaries in the most meaningful life relationships, on the other, run as consistent subtexts throughout all these conversations about remembered and projected domesticity.

NOTES

1. The racial identity of birth fathers was 65% African or African American, 27% European American, 6% Asian, and 2% African American and Native American.

2. The racial identity of birth mothers was 54% European American, 19% Japanese and Korean, 13% African American, 9% mixed race Caribbean Islander, and 4% African American and Native American. See Table II.

3. Birth parents' marital relationship during project participants' childhood: 46% married, 15% never married, 33% divorced, 6% dissolved by death.

4. Of the childhood care-giving parents, one mother never married, 35 (67%) married once, 8 (15.5%) married twice, and 8 (15.5%) married thrice; the mother's marriage to the father was her first in 43 instances (83%), her second in 6 (12%), her third in 1 (2%), and unknown in 2 (3%). Twenty-five (48%) fathers married once, 17 (33%) twice, 7 (13%) thrice, and 3 (6%) an unknown number of times. The father's marriage to the offspring's mother was his first in 37 instances (71%), his second in 10 (19%), his third in 1 (2%), and unknown in 4 (8%).

5. Parents with professional occupations: 42 (80%) fathers; 30 (58%) mothers. See Table III.

6. See Table IV.

7. To identify these and other voices, see Table XX in Part II.

8. See Table V.

9. Among these Biracial young adults, 17 (52%) females and 5 (26%) males said that they did not share feelings about race with anyone while growing up.

10. 41 (79%) project participants have siblings; 18 (35%) have younger siblings, 14 (27%) have older siblings, and 9 (17%) have both older and younger siblings.

11. Born outside the United States: 9 (17%); overseas experience: 30 (58%).

12. See Table VI.

13. Close relationships with mother's family, 21 (40%); with father's family, 10 (19%); or with both parents' families, 6 (12%). Close relationships with maternal families of color, 12, and with maternal European American families, 15; with paternal families of color, 12, and with paternal European American families, 4.

14. No relationship with father's family, 13 (25%) and no relationship with mother's family, 3 (6%). Racial identity of grandparents with whom have no relationship: African American, 6 (12%), European American, 5 (10%), Asian, 5 (10%).

15. 37% married or partnered. Of the 19 who are married: 32% married to a Biracial person, 32% to a European American, 21% to an African American or Black person, 15% to a Latino American. See Table VII.

16. Two of these men are African American/Asian, the other man is African American/European American, and the woman is African American/European.

17. See Table VIII.

Biracial American Identity Choices

3

Americans become aware of race as a social identity at different ages.[1] While children of color become aware of racial differences earlier than European American children, there is considerable variation among all children in their developing racial consciousness. Biracial Americans also come to an awareness of racial identity at different times in their childhood. In response to situations occurring inside and outside their homes, Biracial Americans develop an appreciation of how they are alike and unlike others with respect to race.

Although their parentage affiliates Biracial Americans with two major "racial" groupings in American society, the racial identities that they claim are varied more complexly than their parentage alone would suggest. Not only do young adult Biracial Americans of similar parentage differ in the racial identity self-descriptors that they select, but individuals often have chosen different racial self-descriptors over time. Many remember experiencing significant turning points in the development of their racial identity. Both social context and psychosocial development contribute to the variety of racial self-identifiers that Biracial Americans say that they use and have used during their lifetimes.

FIRST MEMORIES OF RACE AS A SOCIAL IDENTITY

"What is your first memory of race as a social identity?" was the initial question that I posed when interviewing young adult Biracial Americans about their memories of race and racial identity during their formative years and their assessment of race in their mature lives. Although some (5, or 10%) Biracial Americans maintained that because they were always aware of race and physical difference, they had no definite first memory, and some (5, or 10%) were unaware of race as a social identity until middle school or later, most focused on an initial experience that occurred in nursery school (8, or 15%), or more typically, in elementary school (34, or 65%).

The range of responses to the initial question about first memories of race is indicated by the following statements. One woman of European American and African American parentage averred, "I would say that I have no first memory. I think that it was built in me from very young—from the womb practically. I think, because race was so important in my household; it was always being discussed; it was always seen as a social, political, economic state of being and I was always African American and I was always Jewish, I was always Biracial" (Voice 43). A European American/African American man recalled an incident in primary school. "I think my first memories of race as a social identity probably center around conflict. And the reason why I say that is I am very fair skinned. . . . I remember one incident when I was leaving school, a boy said to me. . . . 'You're White.' . . . I was very upset and I told him, 'No, no, I'm Black; you're wrong'" (Voice 38). A woman of Asian/European American parentage recalled,

We lived in an all-White town . . . [with] a really small Chinese community. . . . When we were really small, we would go to these Chinese [Association] parties. We were always the only kids who had a White parent. And everyone there could speak Chinese, . . . we were the only ones that couldn't. . . . In the White context, probably sometime early in school when kids would always ask me, "Are you adopted?" or say, "You are adopted," because my mom would always take us to school. (Voice 36)

Finally, a European American/African American man said, "I remember distinctly when I was very little, my mom said to me, 'You're Black.' She said, 'I'm your mother and legally that makes you Black'" (Voice 31). Although these recollections refer to early childhood experiences,

Table IX
First Memory of Race as a Social Identity

None (always aware of racial differences):	5 (10%)
Aware Appearance Differed from Others:	12 (23%)
Experienced Racial Slurs:	14 (27%)
Experienced Differential Treatment:	11 (21%)
Experienced Physical Conflict with Peers:	4 (7%)
Received Positive Parental Instruction:	3 (6%)
Experienced Race-based Cliques:	3 (6%)

some respondents recalled that their initial awareness of race as a social identity occurred later in their lives.[2]

Many individuals said that this initial experience of race as a social identity was an awareness that they looked different from other children, a recollection of enduring racial slurs from peers, a remembrance of receiving differential treatment from peers and sometimes adults, a memory of physical conflict with peers around racial issues, a reminiscence of positive parental instruction about their heritages, and a memory of dilemmas created by race-based peer cliques.[3] One African American/Asian woman, for example, recalled a early childhood dispute with her Biracial cousins about racial identity. "When I was probably six or seven years old, . . . my cousins who are half Korean and half Black . . . didn't want to believe that they were Black at all. So we had this big fight and big discussion over who was Black and who wasn't. That's when my identity [awareness] came that I was Black and I was proud of it. They were in tears, because they were Black" (Voice 19). Another woman of African American/European American parentage remembered making a difficult lunchroom choice between friends. "The first time that I went to school . . . the tables in the lunchroom were segregated . . . by choice. I can remember this . . . [Black] girl saying, 'Aren't you going to sit with us?' And being torn, because I was with Kim, who was White and a good friend of mine. . . . And I chose to sit at the White table and I can remember feeling really ill about that" (Voice 24). Many years later, then, these women, like others with whom I spoke, recalled the interpersonal and internal conflicts that gave rise to their consciousness of race as a social identity.

CURRENT RACIAL IDENTITY CHOICES

In theory and in practice, Biracial Americans can choose to identify publicly with both, with one, or with none of their racial heritages.

Table X
Current Racial Self-Identity Choices

SINGLE DESCRIPTORS

Monoracial Identity of Color:	**25 (48%)**
Biracial or Multiracial Identity:	**11 (21%)**
Raceless Identity:	**6 (12%)**

MULTIPLE DESCRIPTORS

Identity of Color & Biracial Identity:	**6 (12%)**
Identity of Color & Raceless Identity:	**3 (5%)**
Raceless Identities:	**1 (2%)**

Most men and women with whom I talked select a single racial self-descriptor (81%); others choose multiple descriptors.[4] Among those using a single self-descriptor, most opt for a monoracial identity of color such as "African American" or "Black"; some for a biracial or multiracial identity such as "Black-and-Korean" or "African American-and-Syrian"; and others for a raceless identity such as "Other" or "Human." Those who currently choose multiple self-descriptors for their racial identity include those claiming both an identity of color and a Biracial identity such as "African American or African American-and-Irish" or "Black or Biracial"; those asserting both an identity of color and an ambiguous or raceless identity such as "Mixed or Other" or "Black-and-Korean or Other," and those, more rarely, choosing raceless self-descriptors like "Other and Unknown."[5] These primary racial self-identity choices of project participants are idiosyncratic, for they are not systematically related to a person's gender, age, or parentage.

In addition to such primary public self-identifications, Biracial Americans acknowledge that they may change their racial self-descriptors in different social contexts. For some, situational relevance is associated with stressing a particular aspect of their racial heritage, while for others disclosing their Biraciality depends on social comfort. For example, one man of European American/African American-Native American parentage said, "I would say that I'm Italian, African American, and American Indian—all three. . . . It depends on the situation. . . . In a lot of the work that I do, I like to refer back to my American Indian heritage, because I do a lot with nature and the environment and that [heritage] is a really good tie-in" (Voice 12). Although, for this man, specifying an aspect of his racial heritage is occupationally useful, others stated that disclosing their Biraciality depended on the social context. One woman of African American/European American parentage explained, "At first I say 'African American' unless I feel that someone has a right to know and then I say, 'Mixed'" (Voice 13). Another woman of African and European American parentage also expressed the significance of social comfort in fully disclosing her racial identity. "Whenever I had to fill out a box, I always checked the 'Black' box. Sometimes I check the 'Black' and 'White' together; it depends on how much latitude I have and where I am. . . . If I were to be specific, I would say 'Nigerian' and . . . what tribe, because I've always thought of myself as 'Black' first, 'Biracial'—if I felt safe enough to say that I was Biracial. But I've never identified myself as 'White'" (Voice 9). Both of these women's statements imply that their Biracial identity is a hidden identity that is revealed only in socially comfortable situations.

Perceptions of both White racism and White cultural identification may contribute to individuals' comfort or discomfort with claiming an identity of color. A woman of African American/Asian parentage explained her perception that racist assumptions make people insist on identifying her as 'Biracial' rather than 'African American.' She said,

I always have [identified myself as "African American"]. I never felt the need to tell anyone I was Japanese, though they always seemed to figure out that I can't be all African American or all Black. They say, "Oh, you can't possibly be." And I've learned that it's a totally racist thing. I never thought anything about it originally, but I've learned that . . . because I'm intelligent, I have to be something other than Black. Because I'm pretty, I have to be something other than Black. . . . A lot of times I say "No, I'm just Black. No, I'm just African American." (Voice 5)

This woman, therefore, asserts a monoracial public identity to counter racist perceptions. By contrast, a woman of African American and European American parentage now identifies with the White culture in which she grew up but for many years felt compelled to identify herself as "Black."

[I identify myself as "Human," but I haven't always identified myself that way.] I've always identified myself as "Black" and I feel really uncomfortable with that. . . . I felt, if anything, I totally identified myself as being "White" . . . having grown up in a White Anglo Saxon Protestant family. . . . So being 'Human' is post-twenty-two [years old]. . . . I actually do talk about myself as being "Brown." It always confounds people, but if I have to tell people what my color is, if I'm going to be literal about it, then I am brown. And I love to say to people, "I'm not 'Black,'" because when people ask you what color you are, they really want to know what your socioeconomic status is, what kind of music you like, do you have money, did you go to school. And I don't think that's anybody's business anyway. (Voice 24)

Although providing different responses to the issue of Biracial identity, both these women express the view that a person's racial self-identity may be arbitrarily ascribed by hegemonic White culture and society; both also oppose this social reality.

DEVELOPMENTAL CHOICES

Most Biracial Americans whom I interviewed assert that they have always claimed their current racial identity (58%), but many have chosen at least one other racial identity in the past. One woman who today describes herself as "Latina" claimed to be "Dominican" and "Mixed" earlier in her life. Another who identifies herself as "Chinese/German American" claimed a raceless identity and next, an "Asian American" identity in the past. One man, who identifies himself as "African American" today, claimed a "White" identity in high school. In roughly equal numbers, individuals have changed from a negative racial identity (such as "Other" or "Unknown") to either a positive affirmation of an iden-

Table XI
Changes in Racial Identity

TO RACIAL IDENTITY	FROM RACIAL IDENTITY			
	Negative Racial Identity	Biracial Identity	Identity Of Color	European American Identity
Positive Identity Of Color	3	3	--	2
Positive Identity Of All Heritages	3	3	1	--
Raceless Identity			2	1
Synonymous Cultural Identity[1]	--	--	4	--

1. For example, from "Black" to "African American."

tity of color or to a positive affirmation of all their racial heritages; from a Biracial identity to a monoracial identity of color or a positive identification with multiple heritages; from a monoracial heritage of color to a cultural identity that is synonymous with that color identity, or that embraces multiple heritages, or that is raceless. Finally, of the three who claimed a European American identity in the past (14%), two have assumed positive monoracial identities of color and one a negative raceless identity.[6] One woman of European American and African American-Native American parentage has used a multiplicity of racial self-descriptors during her lifetime.

I used to say, "I'm 'Mixed,'" and people would say, "With what?" And I'd say, "Black and White." And I think that I stayed "Black and White" for a long time, though when I was pretending I was Puerto Rican, I told people I was "Puerto Rican." And there was a time when I felt . . . so much shame about my race and so much insecurity that I told people I was "Spanish." . . . And I went back to being "Black and White." And I guess the more politicized and educated [you become], . . . you go through this whole process of terminology. So I started to be "African American and Jewish." . . . So then it developed into "European American and African American." And then I think it was my mother sort of strongly asserting her Native American lineage. . . . And then I felt I could claim that as well. (Voice 43)

The myriad changes in this woman's racial self-descriptors were related not only to her peripatetic childhood, in which she changed communities and schools every couple of years, but to her evolving sociopolitical sophistication. While her multiplicity of racial self-descriptors over time is noteworthy, many people have changed self-descriptors more than once during their lifetimes.

Motivations for changing racial self-descriptors vary. Some people attribute changes in childhood and adolescence to a sense of difference and shame about their Biraciality. One woman of European American and Afro-Latino parentage proudly proclaims her "Dominican" identity today. "[But] at that stage—fifth to eighth grade, I was White. I was ashamed of being Hispanic. . . . And then again I became ashamed of being White in high school—not so much ashamed, just totally disinterested and . . . I didn't even acknowledge that side of me. And I still kind of don't. I don't feel Jewish at all—I don't relate to that at all" (Voice 30). For a few, this sense of confusion persists into adulthood, as one African American/European American woman poignantly related. "I've lied for many years. I've said I was 'White'—Italian. But on any application or anything, I always put 'Other.' And I felt if they wanted to know enough, they would ask me. I never really knew what to put, sometimes I used 'Black and White,' and basically, now, 'Unknown'—I don't know what I am" (Voice 40). Although this woman's claiming of a raceless identity stems from confusion about racial identity, others may assume a raceless identity from a conscious lack of interest in claiming a racial identity. Thus, one African American/European American man stated "I don't identify myself racially—only my parents' respective races. If asked, I'll say, 'Well, my grandmother came from the Soviet Union and my father is an African American.' I went through a couple of periods of saying 'I'm Black; I'm African American' and periods of saying 'I'm African American/Jewish'" (Voice 33).

Individuals variously relate how they came to view themselves as "Black" or "African American." One woman articulates the view that American Blacks encompass Biracial Americans who have a partial African American heritage.

I identified myself for many years as "Other" on those checklists and as "Mixed Race" and as "Biracial"—trying to find a way to define myself which is not afforded. But I do feel comfortable calling myself "Black." . . . In my historical context, I am Black and the kind of Black I am, my specific Black experience, is as mixed race—I had a White mother and a Black father. And I think that's the best way to explain it, because there are so many different ways of being Black. And the myth is the . . . homogenized Black community. There are so many different kinds of Black people and Black experiences. It also helps me to claim my experience as a Black experience. (Voice 1)

Another woman delineates her reasons for preferring "African American" to "Black" today.

[I've identified myself] always as Black [and now] African American as part of trying to think about ethnicity more than race. It's part of my whole thing about language is really important and how you use language really does make a difference and words have meaning. So I think in some ways "African American" better tells who I am in terms of my origin as a person, both in terms of stereotypes and within my family—rich kind of family Afro origins, but also American origins within America as a country of a conglomeration of folks, and the race dynamic—black, white are colors. Really, people are defining me because of my skin tone and I'd rather be defined because of my background. (Voice 41)

For others, affirming a racial identity of color or a Biracial identity stems from increasing personal comfort with their racial identity. One

African American/European American woman who as an adolescent was confused about how to label her racial identity said, "In college . . . I found myself leaning toward defining myself as an African American woman, though I always find myself qualifying that whenever someone asks me [about my racial identity], and I always add on 'but I come from a Biracial background.' And even now, there's not a term for me . . . that puts these two worlds together" (Voice 29). An African American/Asian woman described how she evolved from a monoracial to a Biracial identity. "I'd always say that I was 'African American.' I always think that I basically felt more American than Japanese. . . . But I always say, 'Oh, my dad's Black and my mom's Japanese.' But on forms that say 'mark one,' I'd always mark 'African American.' In high school, . . . I felt, 'well, I'm one half; my mother's . . . a part of me, I'm a part of her' . . . that's when I started saying 'Afro-Amerasian' or 'African Asian American'" (Voice 5).

As these statements indicate, cultural identities and affinities, social situations and personal relationships, cognitive reflections and perceived societal demands variously contribute to changing racial self-identities during Biracial Americans' psychosocial maturation. George Kitahara Kich has defined three stages in Biracial identity development: preadolescent awareness of difference, adolescent struggle for others' acceptance, and adult self-acceptance as a person with Biracial and bicultural identity (Kich 1992: 305). "[T]he biracial person's ability to create congruent self-definitions rather than be determined by others' definitions and stereotypes may be said to be the major achievement of a biracial and bicultural identity (Kich 1992: 314)." Although some of the Biracial young adults in this study continue to struggle to achieve self-acceptance, most have developed a self-affirming racial identity.

SIBLINGS' RACIAL IDENTITY CHOICES

Among the young Biracial Americans with whom I talked were nine sets of siblings. Twenty of the fifty-two project participants had a brother or a sister who was also interviewed.[7] Except for one brother and sister who hold divergent racial self-identities today—she a monoracial identity of color and he a Biracial identity—the members of all the other sibling groups have chosen the same racial identity. Most have chosen a monoracial identity of color, while three siblings identify themselves as Biracial.

Although the siblings with whom I talked have assumed similar adult racial identities, the age at which they first became aware of race as a social identity often differed. One sister said that she first became aware of race in elementary school, while her younger sister asserted that she had always been aware of race. Another woman became conscious of race as a social identity in nursery school, while her younger brothers did not achieve such awareness until elementary and middle school. Yet another woman claimed to have been always aware of race, while her younger sister remembered first being aware in elementary school.

Whereas some siblings became aware of racial identity issues without any remembered precipitating experience, many recalled peer rejection expressed through slurs and fights in elementary school or race-based peer cliques in middle school. One woman—whose two younger brothers recalled elementary school fights and middle school cliques—remembered teachers speaking to her in Korean rather than in English in nursery school, which made her feel different from other children. Thus, even children growing up within the same household may become aware of racial identity issues at different times in their lives, because of their distinctive childhood experiences outside their homes.

TURNING POINTS

Just as there are some Biracial Americans who have no first memory of race, there are some who do not consider that they have experienced any turning point in the development of their racial identity. The vast majority, however, recall at least one turning point and many have experienced several. By "turning point," I refer to an experience that either alters a person's racial self-identity or strengthens their racial self-identity construct. Of those who have experienced turning points, most remember their first during their preteen years, some in high school or in college, and a few after college. Most associated turning points with changing communities (57%)—moving from the city to the suburbs, living in another country, going to a new school, or starting college. Others acknowledge a heightened awareness of difference at certain times in their lives (30%). Several recall a specific, painful experience of racial rejection (13%) from a parent, from a shopkeeper, from a peer, or from a colleague.

One African American/Asian woman recalled an early childhood experience that dramatically established her sense of racial identity.

[During] the [1968] riots in Chicago, I was with my mother. My mother is Japanese and so she would go across that border line . . . [to] a shoe shop that she liked. I remember going with her one day when all this stuff was going on and being in this shoe shop and some guy came in just ranting and raving, "Niggers this and niggers that." . . . He looked at me and he looked at my mother; he asked her, "She ain't no nigger is she?" And my mother's face just turned and she was so scared, and I wasn't scared. . . . I remember my mother's face and I thought that I would never deny my heritage or never be ashamed of it; never allow anyone to make it an issue for me. . . . I couldn't have been more than eight years old. (Voice 5)

Others associated important turning points with moving away from home either to begin work in a new community or to attend college. One African American/Asian man described his quest for a meaningful racial identity in the years after he left high school. He said, "[When I got out of high school,] I started to dance for the stage. So I went to New York and stayed there. That was my first experience with Blacks other than my own family. . . . That was the turning point for me. . . . Between that time [and when I was twenty-six], I searched for who I was. I went back and forth a lot between [cultures]. . . . So, . . . I decided, 'well, I'm just "Afro-Asian," that's who I am'" (Voice 8).

A woman of African/European American parentage described the turning points she experienced in leaving a rural European American community for college.

But I think the most significant thing was coming to college—coming to Boston, because it was the first time that I was around Black people. And then being Black in Boston and all that that means, and I had no idea of what being African American was at all; I didn't have any of the cultural references, I didn't have any of the language. I knew how to interpret overt racism, but I didn't know how to interpret much of the subtle stuff that goes on. . . . I think I'd always thought of myself as a woman of color—or at least half woman of color—and when I came here, I didn't feel African American and I also realized that this little dream I'd carried around of being African when I was reunited with Africans wasn't going to work. . . . So I had to stop thinking of myself as African and try to think of myself as African American very slowly. After I graduated, I ended up going to Finland and while I was there with my relatives, somebody asked me a question that I couldn't answer and they said, "Gee, it doesn't seem like you're very interested in your Scandinavian heritage." And then it occurred to me . . . [that] since I left home, I haven't really thought of myself as Scandinavian any more, because it's not really a source of comfort. . . . And it occurred to me that I had moved away from the White side of my family and what was I going to be next? And then . . . I started getting involved with the Nigerian expatriate community . . . I went to Nigeria. Going to Africa, meeting my family, led to whatever that was. And now I'm trying to integrate it all. (Voice 9)

A man of European American and Afro-Caribbean parentage related how his collegiate experience heightened his racial identity awareness.

Well, it was at Stanford that even sense of humor and the way people like to spend time and the way they thought about their family connections and their friends and their work life—on all those dimensions [I discovered] that I was not White. . . . Then I realized that your choices of where to spend time when you're truly in a mixed setting can be so political. And there was a tendency of people—given my complexion—to pull me in. . . . There was a tendency either to consider me Latino . . . or any way White enough to include in the activities . . . and [on] the flip side I began to be conscious of how I had a connection to and an understanding of the Latino and Black students that the White peers often did not have. (Voice 15)

Finally, a woman of African American and European American parentage described the turning point that she experienced in late adolescence and her perception of the meaning of being a Biracial American.

I think the most formative experience for me was learning [that] both White people and Black people cut you down. . . . I learned it from the White side when I was a senior in high school and I learned that as a freshman and a sophomore in college from the Black side. So in that three-year span I had the experiences which made me have to carve out a racial identity that bound my duality and becoming comfortable with that, because both sides—Black and White—weren't going to be comfortable with my duality. . . . The White world was going to have problems around me, because despite the fact that I was intelligent . . . , I was Black. . . . The White people that I interacted with in [my home town] really at some level . . . had been able to develop relationships with me and have friendships with me, because they could forget that I was Black, instead of embracing that as part of who I was. . . . And then from the Black viewpoint, Blacks will continually use my status as a Biracial person as a way to attack me or as a way to explain why I could have a perspective that is different from theirs that they didn't think was right or to explain why I didn't fit into their own self-stereotypes of how they or they how Black people generally should be. So people literally say things to me like, "You just can't understand, because you're White." And actually not knowing that probably I could understand more . . . than they could understand, because they don't have that duality in their life, to manage, to think about, to sort through. (Voice 41)

As these selections suggest, for most Biracial Americans, racial identity evolves and changes over time. Today most of the Biracial young adults with whom I spoke publicly claim a monoracial identity of color (48%); many, a Biracial identity (21%), and a few, a raceless identity (14%). Others use more than one self-descriptor—identifying themselves monoracially and biracially or biracially and ambiguously (17%). The racial identity that most individuals proudly claim today, however, is often not the one that they have always claimed. One woman who today identifies herself as "Hispanic" spent her middle-school years as "European American." One man who considers himself "African American/German American" said that between the ages of thirteen and twenty-one, he found his racial identity so painful to contemplate that he considered himself only as an individual devoid of race; several women and men mentioned that they had identified themselves as European Americans earlier in their lives and now claim an identity of color, and one man who had once called himself "Black" now does not identify with any racial category.

CONCLUSION

For Biracial Americans, racial self-identity constructs often vary over time and in different social contexts. (See chapter 6 for additional information about memories of racial identity issues.) Perhaps one of the most historically distinctive aspects of the post–Civil Rights generation of Biracial Americans' experience is its ability to publicly claim its biraciality. Some perceive this ability to be more available to the next generation of Biracial Americans than to their own generation. The post–Civil Rights generation of Biracial Americans represented by the young adults in this study, then, is a transitional generation of Biracial Americans between the hidden generations of the past and the subsequent openly blended generation. One African American/European American woman observed, "I think it's interesting that this cohort of Biracial kids who are five or so years younger than I am check off 'Black and White' or 'Asian and White' or 'Hispanic and White' on their forms. It's a whole different way of constructing yourself than anything I would ever have thought of. . . . My conception of myself is that I'm a Black person; that's just who I am" (Voice 41). Nevertheless, this perception of the growing freedom of Biracial youth to claim their multiracial heritage publicly and the ability of the post–Civil Rights generation to construct racial self-identities that are diverse and personally efficacious are historically important developments in the Biracial American experience.[8]

NOTES

1. For an insightful contemporary discussion of racial identity development, see Beverly Daniel Tatum, *"Why Are All the Black Kids Sitting Together in the Cafeteria?" And Other Conversations About Race.* New York: Basic Books, 1997.

2. Voices are identified in Table XX in Part II.

3. See Table IX.

4. For recent insightful discussions of racial identity choices, see Cookie White Stephan, "Mixed-Heritage Individuals: Ethnic Identity and Trait Characteristics," in Root 1992: 50–63 and Theresa Kay Williams, "Race as Process: Reassessing the 'What Are You?' Encounters of Biracial Individuals," in Root 1996: 191–210.

5. See Table X.

6. See Table XI.

7. Among the project participants are seven sets of two siblings each and two sets of three siblings each.

8. For an interesting discussion of "this new blended identity" among University of California students, see G. Reginald Daniel, "Black and White Identity in the New Millennium: Unsevering the Ties that Bind," in Root (1996): 121–139.

4

Racial Realities in Adult Biracial American Lives

Young adult Biracial Americans have divergent perceptions of their Biracial status as well as varying views of the significance of race in their adult lives. Moreover, some of these perceptual differences are gendered. Biracial American men and women, then, hold similar but also different understandings about the role of race in their adult lives. In this chapter I explore not only perceptions of Biracial status but assessments of the role of race in certain important life choices.

PERCEPTIONS OF BIRACIAL STATUS

While most Biracial Americans readily acknowledge their biraciality, some do not identify themselves as Biracial persons. Their reasons for eschewing Biracial status range from the political and philosophical to the personal. Two men of European American and African American parentage give divergent explanations for why they avoid identifying themselves as Biracial people. The first asserts, "I don't really believe in biraciality per se, in that more than any of the [other] social constructs, biraciality is a social construct. . . . I will be Black until the race problem is done" (Voice 31). The second states, "I don't consider myself Biracial, because . . . all of us share such a diverse gene pool and so many African Americans have a broader gene pool than that name connotes. . . . By the same token, there are many people who consider themselves to be White and of European ancestry that have such diverse genes way back there. . . . so I would not label myself 'Biracial'" (Voice 38). In identifying themselves as African Americans rather than as Biracial people, one man's reasons are essentially political; the other's, biosocial.[1]

Deciding to identify only with one's heritage of color or only with one's European American heritage may derive from very personal circumstances. One young woman, for example, who grew up with her European American mother without ever knowing her African American father or his relatives stated, "I don't have a Biracial heritage—I have a White heritage," (Voice 24) whereas another woman who strongly rejected her European American father after her parents' divorce said, "I consider myself Hispanic" (Voice 37).

To disavow biraciality as a self-construct, however, need not mean denying the reality of one's parents' different racial affiliations. One European American/African American man continued, "I would not label myself 'Biracial,' but the obvious social reality is that my father was White and my mother is Black" (Voice 38). While political identification with the heritage of color, biosocial recognition of human genetic diversity, or personal rejection of a parent may preclude affirming a Biracial social identity, individuals can still acknowledge their parents' socially constructed racial differences.

The vast majority (90%) of these Biracial young adults, however, fully acknowledge and variously assess their Biracial heritage.[2] As adults, both men and women take pride and comfort in their Biraciality. One European American/Afro-Caribbean man observed, "I consider my Biracial ancestry an asset in terms of living well, enjoying my life, and having a sense of place. . . . I can straddle [different cultural worlds]

Table XII
Perceived Assets of Biraciality as Adults

ASSETS	WOMEN	MEN
Do Not Identify As Biracial	3 (10%)	2 (10%)
Pride	10 (35%)	6 (32%)
Cross-Cultural Skills	10 (35%)	6 (32%)
Not Easily Labeled	2 (7%)	3 (16%)
Being Unique	2 (7%)	0
Hyperrealized Racial Sense	1 (3%)	0
Color Privilege	1 (3%)	0
Less Prejudiced	0	1 (5%)
None	0	1 (5%)

Table XIII
Perceived Liabilities of Biraciality as Adults

LIABILITIES	WOMEN	MEN
Not Belonging to Single Race	10 (59%)	3 (22%)
African Americans' Liabilities	2 (11%)	1 (7%)
Fear of Rejection	1 (6%)	1 (7%)
Feel Must Educate Blacks and Whites	1 (6%)	0
Rejection by Blacks	1 (6%)	3 (22%)
Rejection by Whites	0	1 (7%)
Rejection by Asians	0	1 (7%)
Pressure to Identify Monoracially	1 (6%)	0
Other	1 (6%)	0
None	0	4 (28%)

and do that comfortably. . . . The asset clearly for me in working is having insight into different cultural worlds . . . and being able to apply those insights" (Voice 15). His views were echoed by an African American/European American woman.

For me being Biracial means I can't make big sweeping statements, because life is very grey. . . . Being Biracial has given me the capacity to work with people whose experiences . . . are extremely different from mine. . . . I have no experience with the kinds of poverty and the kinds of family structure that my clients have, but I really do understand at some level the feeling of not having a place where you fit in and . . . feeling judged and prejudged because of who people perceive you to be. (Voice 41)

A European American/African American woman considered that "[Being Biracial] is a wonderful asset; it allows us to communicate with so many different people and to understand that the differences between races or cultures or sexual identities . . . are really differences of language and posture" (Voice 43). These young adult Biracial Americans, like others with whom I spoke, value not only their ability to move comfortably within and between different cultures but their insights into different cultural worlds, which they perceive derive from their multicultural experiences as Biracial Americans. Occasionally, individuals mention that their own status as outsiders gives them insights into situations of others whose differences emanate not from race but from other sources, such as poverty or sexual identity preferences.

Another positive aspect of their biraciality that several women and men appreciate is others' inability to readily classify them racially. One

Table XIV
Perceived Privileges of Biraciality as Adults

PRIVILEGES	WOMEN	MEN
None	2 (12%)	3 (21%)
Light Skin Tone	7 (44%)	1 (7%)
Employment Opportunities	3 (19%)	5 (36%)
Cross-Cultural Skills/Insights	1 (6%)	1 (7%)
Other	3 (19%)	4 (29%)

African American/Asian man, for example, said, "When you meet people, they can't immediately pigeonhole you. When I meet a person, clearly they notice that I'm not White but they don't identify me as Black. And that confuses them" (Voice 26). Similarly, a woman of Asian/Afro-Caribbean parentage observed "[As a Biracial person] you can play a lot of games. It's a lot about power. It's a lot about being able to move in a lot of different circles. You avoid being labeled pretty easily, which is one thing I feel pretty strongly about" (Voice 30). Thus, Biracial Americans' ambiguous racial identities enable them to confound assumptions about color categories that many Americans hold.

While men and women share positive assessments of being Biracial, gendered differences emerge in their perceptions of liabilities associated with their mixed race status. Most women (59%) cite not belonging to one racial group as a disadvantage associated with biraciality, whereas many men (36%) cite racial rejection by monoracial people as a major liability. One European American/African American woman stated, "I think that until we really cultivate an alternative community for ourselves, we're very lonely. I've gone through lots of periods of feeling very much like an outcast and not belonging to any group and feeling strangely off-balance. . . . It's that feeling of not having a sort of cultural and visible place and that's very hard" (Voice 11). A woman of African American and Asian parentage observed, "I feel that the only problem is you can't get full acceptance from either side," (Voice 39) while an African American /European American woman said, "[My biraciality] holds me back from joining in, because I don't quite feel like I belong to either culture. Because of my skin color, it's much easier to fit into the White society, so a lot of things I do are dictated by that" (Voice 40).

From a slightly different perspective, an African American/European American man lamented, "I yearn to be accepted to this day. And sometimes in social settings . . . I may become quieter . . . . I have strong concerns for how people view me" (Voice 20). This man's concerns about

Table XV
Perceived Problems of Biraciality as Adults

PROBLEMS	WOMEN	MEN
None	5 (28%)	3 (23%)
Need to Combat Racism	3 (16%)	4 (31%)
Job Discrimination	5 (28%)	2 (15%)
Exoticism	0	2 (15%)
Special Bond with Mixed Race People	1 (5.6%)	0
Rejection by Blacks	1 (5.6%)	2 (15%)
Rejection by Whites	1 (5.6%)	0
Rejection by Asians	1 (5.6%)	0
Dating	1 (5.6%)	0

rejection were echoed by a man of European American and African American parentage. The latter stated, "Today I still have times when I wish that I could fit in more . . . with other Black folks. . . . Folks who are lighter are often perceived as being aloof and a bit snobbish about their social status. I've always made a concerted effort not to appear that way, but it's still an issue that comes up" (Voice 38). Although most men and women perceive liabilities associated with their biraciality, quite a few men (28%) do not perceive any liabilities in their mature lives.

When considering privileges and problems associated with being Biracial young adults, many women cite light skin color as a privilege (44%), whereas many men (36%) stress employment opportunities. In thinking about problems, men mention combating racism (31%) more frequently than women, whereas women cite job discrimination more frequently than men.

In discussing privileges associated with biraciality in their adult lives, women emphasize appearance issues and men, employment opportunities. For example, one European American/African American woman stated, "In so many little ways I receive privileges that other people don't—from the way that my hair looks, to the color that I am, to my features" (Voice 43). Another African American/European American woman also noted that her appearance made it easier to make friends with people "of different colors and backgrounds; once they get to know me, my friends say, 'Wow, I can tell you're really Black.' But at the beginning—it's not making them feel uncomfortable. It's just kind of a generic look. Some people think I'm Jewish, . . . I don't know if it works as well in the African American community where I can just . . . pass" (Voice 6). Although women stress appearance issues and men, economic issues, these issues probably are linked for men, as the following statements suggest. One Asian Caribbean/Afro-Caribbean man said, "The company I work for is a family-owned business. . . . Everybody and their grandmother's in line waiting for an opening within that company and due to my appearance more than anything else when I interviewed with them, it was pretty much a given. . . . The chemistry was there, because of my appearance. . . . they never really had a Black representative" (Voice 21). Another African American/European American man believed that he got a counseling job at the University of California because he was Biracial. "[O]ut of eighty candidates, I was chosen and I was the one who didn't have the prior experience, but I made it pretty clearly known that because of my Biracial background that I was able to attract different groups" (Voice 20). Thus, Biracial young adults' appearance is considered a privilege for both men and women, but men link appearance to economic opportunities more often than do women.

In addition to acknowledging certain privileges associated with their Biracial status, these young adults also readily describe encounters with racism and discrimination. Both men and women experience such encounters in the workplace and in informal settings, involving situations around hiring and promotion and around leisure activities. In certain situations, race is inappropriately denied; in others it is insensitively emphasized. Moreover, these situations arise with people of color as well as with European Americans.

One man of European American and African American parentage described his situation as a teacher in an independent school where his racial identity influenced not only his hiring but his role as Black spokesperson within the school.

It's painful at times . . . being expected to be a spokesperson. . . . There's a lot of racism; people think that they're helping me when they're not. My [prep school] department chair my first year thought he was complimenting me when he told me that, "Hey, you know, if you hadn't been Black and from Harvard, we probably wouldn't have given you a second look." . . . Or making sure that if a Black candidate [for a position at the school] came, I was the person they saw; the right reason for doing that would be just so that I could talk to them, get a sense of who they are. [T]hey [the school] wanted them to know that there was another Black person. . . . I don't like to deal with that stuff; that's just the way it is. I don't blame anybody, but it still hurts; it's part of the Black experience. (Voice 44)

This man, whose racial identity was inappropriately emphasized in the workplace, described an experience of institutional racism.

Two African American/Asian women recounted their experiences of racism in the workplace. One described how she was passed over for a job in favor of a less qualified man; she reflected, "At that time I thought that part of it was because they really weren't ready to have a Black woman running the office that handled all the money that came through the school" (Voice 5). The other woman related an experience associated with a job interview during a job search; she talked with the employer on the telephone and, "we had a great conversation. He must have pictured me as someone else, because when I got to the interview, I was sitting in the waiting room . . . [with] another White woman and he went right to her and said 'Susan, Ms. Schon.' . . . I just thought, 'Well, that was pretty ignorant.' And that was one of the first times that I felt the impact of preconceived ideas in people's minds in a job situation" (Voice 7). The workplace encounters that these women describe have overtones of sexism as well as racism.

Light skin presents both privileges and problems in Biracial Americans' relations to both European Americans and people of color. On the one hand, many Biracial Americans perceive that European Americans are more comfortable interacting with them as light-skinned people of color than with darker skinned people of color. In certain social contexts even today, Biracial Americans who are partly of African American descent may have a privileged status within African American society. This was recognized by a light skinned European American/African American man. "I think there may be some social advantage, especially in the sort of social circles that I travel in now—the young professional Black people who still hold some ideas about what are . . . desirable physical attributes in terms of hair and skin color" (Voice 38). Certainly the historically privileged position that mulattoes enjoyed in American society has been eloquently recorded by Edward Byron Reuter in *The Mulatto in the United States* (1918). On the other hand, the light skin that is a source of privilege is also a source of conflict, especially among monoracial people of color. Biracial American project participants often spoke of the way in which African Americans and Asians challenged their identity as people of color, especially in informal settings. Nevertheless, one African American/European American woman argued that within the workplace,

[t]he issues of color consciousness among African Americans comes less into play for your mobility within the structure, because the structure tends to be dominated by Whites. So the discussion tends to come about how Whites deal with you, because they're in the power structure positions and they hinder your mobility. I definitely think whether it's in a work context or a social con-

text that people who are Biracial or even just the issue if you're a light-skinned African American or a dark-skinned African American—there's a whole lot of intraracial stuff that goes on, it's deep, it's complex. (Voice 29)

Although most European Americans are not aware of biraciality as a meaningful social category, in certain workplaces being Biracial may be perceived as an exotic diversity attribute. One African American/European American woman described how in her community service office, European Americans prized Biraciality to the bemusement of the staff members of color.

One of the first things that they would say about [a job candidate] is, "She's Japanese and African American" or "she's African American and White." It was really a [big] thing for White staff to have a Biracial person come in. And we . . . folks of color used to . . . talk about that and say, "What is it?" Because in some respects we're lighter skinned so it's easier to relate to us because visually there isn't so much difference. (Voice 41)

Being light skinned makes Biracial Americans less threatening to Whites than darker people of color and, some say, enables them to be taken more seriously in the workplace. One European American/African American woman concluded, "Maybe because people feel less threatened by me, . . . people do listen when I talk. . . . [I'm] not dismissed as easily." (Voice 29)

How individuals choose to respond to racist experiences depends on contextual considerations. In any given situation, potential strategic responses include confrontation, disregarding, and avoidance. A person may choose to confront the racist incident by challenging its assumptions or perceptions, a person may decide to disregard an incident in pursuit of some more significant goal, and a person may determine that they prefer to avoid any challenging of racist encounters. Which strategic response is selected depends on multiple factors including the content of the racist encounter, the predilections of the individual, and the social context. Although an individual probably prefers one or another of these strategies, a person may use all of them in different social situations.

LIFE CHOICES AND RACE

As young adults, the Biracial Americans whom I interviewed have made important choices about where they wish to live, about their careers, and about friendships and intimate relationships. When asked about the role of race in making these significant life choices, men and women responded with slightly different emphases.

Although most Biracial Americans (54%) stated that they would prefer to live in a racially and ethnically diverse community, this preference was stronger among women (59%) than men (44%).[3] Moreover, more men (34%) than women (16%) preferred to live in a monoracial community—either an African American community or a European American community. Both women and men who have children of their own often cite their children's education as an important consideration in their choice of residential community.

The range of views that these young adult Biracial Americans held about residential communities and the reasons for their choices were variously articulated. A European American/African American man said that his artistic career had "pretty much dictated my placement. I am in a predominantly White rural environment, because it's nice out here." Next year, he said, "I will probably either go back to Philadelphia or . . . down to D.C., where I will probably seek the Black community to live" (Voice 45). A woman of European American and Afro-Latino parentage commented that she liked being in a multiracial community—"I like being around different kinds of people. I don't like being around any one group. I don't want to be in an all-Black neighborhood, an all-White neighborhood, an all-Latino neighborhood. And part of it is [due to] my racial identity and part of it is [due to] growing up in Manhattan" (Voice 37). An African American/European American woman explained her move to the city—"I just couldn't take another year of living in White suburbia. . . . The city for me is reality—it is what the world is. . . . I just think all the dynamics that are both positive and negative about society slap you in the face every day when you live in the city and I like that" (Voice 41). In contrast, an African American/European American man maintained, "I know that I don't

Table XVI
Adult Choices of Residential Communities

TYPE OF COMMUNITY PREFERRED	PROJECT PARTICIPANTS	
	MEN	WOMEN
Racially Diverse Community:	8 (44%)	19 (59%)
African American Community:	3 (17%)	3 (10%)
Middle-Class Community:	2 (11%)	1 (3%)
European American Community:	3 (17%)	2 (6%)
Urban Community:	---	2 (6%)
Not Boston:	---	1 (3%)
West Indies:	---	1 (3%)
No Preference Yet:	2 (11%)	3 (10%)

want to live in Black neighborhoods; I could live in a White neighborhood, though" (Voice 33). Finally, another African American/European American woman explained her move to an urban neighborhood. "I was very conscious . . . of wanting my son to be in a school system where there were more African American kids; I didn't want him to have an experience like I had [growing up in a White suburb]. But I wanted him to be in a very good school system. [This community] met those needs, but I think . . . it's a rare mix where you find quality education and diversity" (Voice 29).

Most respondents say that they wish to live in a racially and culturally diverse community, which often means an urban community. Nevertheless, the desire for a good school system for children or the demands of a career may override the preference for such a community. For some of these young adult Biracial Americans, then, issues of class and community services may supercede a stated preference for an ethnically diverse residential community.

In exploring the relationship between race and work in their lives, Biracial men and women held both similar and divergent views. Many men (35%) and women (34%) with whom I talked said that they would prefer to work in a racially mixed workplace.[4] An Asian/European American woman maintained, "In terms of survival, I feel that I need to look at places that . . . have diversity as a priority in the way that they run their business" (Voice 36). Another woman of European American and Afro-Latino parentage said

I like to see different kinds of people. And in terms of my work, I have chosen work environments accordingly. . . . Since I went to law school, I worked in one place . . . where I was the only Hispanic and there were a handful of African Americans. I worked for City Hall, but the agency I happened to work in had a

Table XVII
Racial Identity and Work

CHOICE OF WORK AND RACE	PROJECT PARTICIPANTS	
	MEN	WOMEN
Not a Factor	6 (35%)	8 (24%)
Work in "White" Setting	2 (12%)	3 (9%)
Race Affects How Does Work	2 (12%)	6 (18%)
Prefer Racially Mixed Workplace	6 (35%)	11 (34%)
Race Affects Work	1 (6%)	3 (9%)
Plan Work Outside USA	--	2 (6%)

majority of women of color. Where I work now is a pretty good mix of people, so that's a very important factor for me in terms of feeling comfortable. (Voice 37)

Some project participants, however, work in predominantly European American milieus (10%). One African American/European American woman, for example, said, "All my positions have been in predominantly White settings, though I have been fortunate to have African American colleagues that I can really confide in. That has made a big difference" (Voice 29). Whether one works in a diverse setting or a predominantly White institution, some Biracial American young adults, especially women, express the importance of supportive network of colleagues of color.

Nevertheless, many men (35%) and women (24%) stated that racial considerations played no part in their choice of work. One man of Asian Caribbean and Afro-Caribbean parentage said, "[With respect to choices of work, my racial identity] is not really the issue; the issue is money. I don't think race has anything to do with it" (Voice 21). Similarly, another man of European American and Afro-Caribbean parentage stated, "In choices of work—[my racial identity] is really a minimal influence. I'm career-oriented enough and interested enough in finding a balance on the residential side that I don't think it influences to a great degree. With other things being equal, I see it as a definite plus to be in a racially mixed workplace" (Voice 15). Contrasting with these views are those held by some for whom racial considerations are extremely significant in their choice of work. One woman of European American and Afro-Latino parentage, for example, stated, "I'm a teacher and I would only want to teach Black and Hispanic kids; I have no desire to teach White kids" (Voice 3). Another African American/European American woman also articulated the significance of racial considerations in her choice of work as a legal advocate. "I knew that I wanted to work with communities of color and low-income communities. . . . My whole way of looking at the world . . . is colored by the fact that I am Biracial, so the decisions I make are all part and parcel of that" (Voice 41). Moreover, quite a number of people noted that race affects the way they do their work.

Thus, while some respondents aver that racial identity issues play no part in their choices of work, many state that their biraciality influences either their choices of work and work settings or the manner in which they do their work. Although African American role models influenced both a poet and a sculptor, the poet considers his racial identity to be central to his work but the sculptor does not perceive that his racial identity influences his art. One law school student perceives that principles of fairness rather than racial identity inform her choices of potential work settings, while a legal advocate thinks that her interest in working with communities of color and low-income people derives from her life experiences as a Biracial person. Others firmly state that race in no way influences their choice of work, whether it be electrical engineering or dating services.

The interplay between racial identity considerations and choice of work is complex. While occupational choice and career orientation may override racial identity considerations, these issues may be perceived as important in the conduct of work and the work setting. In their responses, women tended to emphasize relational aspects in the workplace, while men more often emphasized their career orientation in discussing race and work choices.

Dating and Friendship Patterns

When asked to consider the role of race in their choice of adult relationships, most men (79%) stated that race had nothing to do with their choice of friends, though many women (35%) expressed a preference for friendships with people of color. Nevertheless, when discussing dating and marriage, most women (55%) and men (60%) preferred to date or were married to people of color.[5] Since the cosmopolitan marriage patterns of project participants and their siblings already have been discussed in chapter 2, I focus on dating and friendship patterns in this section.[6]

Just as young adult Biracial Americans are cosmopolitan in their marital choices, so are they universalistic in their friendship and dating relationships. Commonality of interest rather than racial identity and openness to cultural differences are mentioned as bases for establishing friendships. One man of African American/Asian parentage, for example, said "The people that I'm closest to, outside of my wife [who is Biracial]—one is half Jewish and half Spanish . . . and [the other is] the guy I lived with in college, who's White. So the people I'm really close with—I think it has less to do with race than with common interests and just a willingness to be hon-

Table XVIII
Racial Identity and Friendships

RACE AND FRIENDSHIPS	PROJECT PARTICIPANTS	
	MEN	WOMEN
Not a Factor	11 (79%)	7 (30%)
Prefer People of Color	3 (21%)	8 (35%)
Prefer Racially Diverse Friends	--	6 (26%)
Prefer European American Friends	--	2 (9%)

Table XIX
Racial Identity and Dating

RACE AND DATING	PROJECT PARTICIPANTS	
	MEN	WOMEN
Prefer to Date Person of Color	3 (37.5%)	5 (45%)
Prefer to Date European American	3 (37.5%)	5 (45%)
No Preference	2 (25%)	1 (10%)

est" (Voice 26). Nevertheless, several women mentioned a protective wariness about establishing friendships because of previous racist encounters. In addition, one woman noted her dislike for being considered exotic, usually by European American men, while another who had limited exposure to African Americans during her childhood preferred to date European Americans. One European American/Afro-Latino woman explained, "One reason I probably don't date White men very much is that I don't like the whole exotic thing. And I find that [with] Latino men—because Latino[s] . . . are so mixed . . . that I'm just one of many. I'm very attracted to people like that who think I'm just normal, but White men tend to be very confused . . . by me. And I've had that experience with Black men and it's as much of a turnoff" (Voice 3).

In seeking to explain the paradox of her general wariness of establishing friendships and her ability to establish deep relationships across racial lines, one African American/European American woman perceptively addressed the issue of the difference between being a Biracial American and being an American of color.

At some level, because of my own experiences, I've developed a wariness about people generally so it takes me a long time to warm up to people and to commit to relationships with folks. It's very hard for me to sort out being Biracial and being a person of color. I am both of those things and both of those things inform the type of people I have relationships with, who I identify with, how I develop relationships with people. I think clearly I don't have a sense of being limited by racial lines about who I can establish and have close and deep relationships with. And so I think probably that perspective is most directly a product of being Biracial rather than a person of color. (Voice 41)

Having grown up in a predominantly White environment, this woman had limited opportunities for interacting with people of color until she went to college. As an adolescent, she experienced some painful incidents of racial rejection by both European Americans and African Americans, which she perceives have led her to be cautious about establishing friendships. Nevertheless, she has close relationships with both people of color and European Americans. She attributes her negative encounters with European Americans to being a person of color but her ability to establish close relationships with both European Americans and people of color to her Biraciality.

When considering dating and making friends, most respondents have moved towards increasing cosmopolitanism. Several state that earlier in their lives, they had dated only people of color and now were open to dating anyone irrespective of race. A few expressed a strong preference for dating a person of color who could understand their experiences as a person of color, and others, for dating a European American. A few people have married or dated a Biracial person who is not of the same Biracial heritage. With respect to establishing friendships as young adults, most respondents mentioned personal qualities and interests as more significant than racial identity. Thus, for these young adult Biracial Americans, racial considerations assume greater significance in choosing residential communities than in making friends or selecting careers and work environments.

CONCLUSION

Contemporary young adult Biracial Americans hold divergent perceptions of their Biracial status and of how race impacts their mature life choices. These differences derive from many existential sources associated with physical appearance, with formative sociocultural experiences, with socioeconomic and ecological factors, with sociopolitical views and values, and with current life circumstances. The complex interaction of such experiential realities in individual lives produces the multifaceted mosaic that constitutes the Biracial American experience in contemporary American life. (See chapter 9 for additional information about perceptions of biraciality.)

NOTES

1. See Table XX in Part II for the identification of voices.
2. For summaries of gendered similarities and differences in assessments, see Tables XII-XV.
3. See Table XVI.
4. See Table XVII.
5. See Tables VII and XIX.
6. See Tables XVIII and XIX.

5

Biracial American Life Themes

In exploring young adult Biracial Americans' memories of racial identity issues during childhood and adolescence as well as their perceptions of the role of race in their lives today, several major life themes emerged that illuminate significant aspects of the Biracial American experience. These life themes fall into two major categories: systemic and personal. The most important systemic life theme is encountering "White" culture, while among the most salient personal life themes are self construct changes, silent struggles, color conundrums, oppression as and by people of color, and cultural negotiations. Although certain themes have been noted in previous chapters, they are the analytical focus of this one.

ENCOUNTERING "WHITE" CULTURE

At the opening of the twenty-first century in America, all Americans encounter European American cultural hegemony. For some this encounter is mediated by other ethnic cultural experiences, but all must deal with European American dominance in our national culture. For Biracial Americans, this encounter can be more complex than for monoracial Americans of color, because they often have an intimate connection to the dominant culture that does not fully embrace them. Among the Biracial young adults with whom I spoke, the vast majority

(81%) had a European American parent; 54% birthmothers and 27% birthfathers were European Americans. In this chapter I explore five aspects of the Biracial encounter with "White" culture: growing up in a "White" environment, identifying with "White" culture, experiencing "White" racism, confronting colorism, and shattering racial stereotypes.

Growing Up in a "White" Environment

Although all Biracial American children necessarily encounter the dominant culture through television programming, their schooling, and overhearing adult conversation, some grow up in White environments. Although a few are adopted by European American couples, Biracial Americans more often live in communities that are demographically European American and culturally "White." Many of the people whom I interviewed grew up in such White environments. At one extreme are those who grew up in rural areas with European American relatives without exposure to their other socioracial heritage and at the other are those who lived with their parents in demographically European American suburbs with some exposure to other cultures. One African/European American woman who grew up in a rural area with her European American mother and maternal grandparents did not meet any Blacks until she entered college at nineteen; one African American/Asian man, whose family was the only "Black" family in a small New England town, did not encounter African American culture until he moved to New York City after high school. Several others spent most of their formative years in small-town European American environments or in European American urban neighborhoods. Others were raised only by their European American mothers in various community settings, without exposure to their other cultural heritages. Isolated from communities of color during childhood and adolescent years, some Biracial Americans perceive themselves to be culturally "White."

Identifying with White Culture

Identifying with European American culture can lead to Biracial Americans' developing complex orientations toward their heritages. One orientation that quite a few (27%) Biracial Americans adopt is not to address their relationship to communities of color and/or to assume a raceless identity. One woman, for example, said that she did not "start thinking about being brown and really having a racial identity until I was about twenty-two." One man stated that between thirteen and twenty-one years of age he thought of himself as devoid of race, because contemplating his Biracial heritage was too problematic; others spoke of not addressing their identity of color until late adolescence. Avoidance of an identity of color, then, is one strategy that Biracial Americans may use when they identify with "White" culture.

Another strategy that light-skinned Biracial Americans may adopt is to identify themselves as racially "White." Several Biracial young adults mentioned that they had "passed" as European Americans. "Passing" differs from experiencing "White-skin privilege," which light-skinned people of color may encounter in public places. "Passing" implies a person of color's intentional strategy in a social situation, while experiencing "White-skin privilege" depends on the attribution of others. In the pre–Civil Rights era, light-skinned African Americans "passed" situationally or for a lifetime to avoid and transcend the worst features of a segregated society—to sit in a comfortable railway car rather than a Jim Crow car in the South or to establish a comfortable professional life in European American society.[1] While historically African Americans tolerated passing as a valid social strategy, in the post–Civil Rights era most African Americans no longer perceive "passing" as a legitimate or necessary strategy. "Passing" today, therefore, often involves the person who uses it in feelings of guilt about denying their Biracial identity.

The ambiguities of such situations are reflected in this African American/European American woman's response to how she identifies herself racially.

I put first "White" and then "Black." If ever I have a choice, I always say that I'm both. But if someone asked me, "Which do you truly identify with?" I would have to say "White." That's mainly because I look White and my friends are White. I mean if I went to a club that was all Black, I might not feel so uncomfortable, but I would rather be in a White setting, because that's how I identify myself. (Voice 42)[2]

While this woman hesitates to deny her Biraciality, she feels more comfortable in a White environment where others perceive her as another European American. She acknowledges that she identifies with White culture, as do several other Biracial Americans in this study.

Experiencing White Racism

Biracial Americans, like other Americans of color, experience White racism in various institutional and interpersonal forms. Racial rejection is a form of interpersonal racism in which a person's identity as a person of color leads another to repulse a significant relationship with the person of color. The White rejecter may be a parent, a grandparent, or a peer. Such rejection is particularly devastating when the rejecter is a beloved person. Several project participants recounted such traumatic childhood experiences, while others described adult experiences in the workplace and in their social lives. One African American/European American woman recalled a stepgrandmother's angry insistence that the woman as a little girl never identify herself as the woman's granddaughter, for "I am not your grandmother!" Another woman of European American/Afro-Latino parentage recalled the psychic pain associated with her paternal grandmother's rejection of her Jewish identification, when she responded to the girl's "Oh, I'm Jewish, too!" with "You're not Jewish."

In addition, many project participants recalled racist incidents involving their peers in childhood and adolescence. Often these incidents involved racial slurs and fights. Several project participants articulated their perceptions about the enduring consequences of such youthful experiences on their feelings about establishing interpersonal relationships. An African American/European American man, for example, attributed his transformation at age ten from an extrovert to an introvert to "issues around my racial identity and people responding to me hostilely for the first time in my life" (Voice 14). As this example suggests, experiences of racial rejection may have long-term consequences for subsequent orientations towards interactions with other people.

Another more subtle form of racial rejection that Biracial Americans who live in White environments may experience is racial denial or failing to acknowledge a person's racial identity. One African American/European American woman recalled her "awful [high school] experiences," when "people would say to me, 'You know, sometimes I forget you're Black.' That's such a shock! Are you really saying that to me? . . . You expect me to say 'Oh, great, I'm glad you can do that'?" (Voice 41). Such racial denial may lead White peers who are close friends to speak derogatorily about people of color with Biracial individuals. By assuming that friendship supercedes race, White peers deny the person of color's racial sensibilities. By being integrated into the White community, the person of color becomes an insider with whom disparaging remarks about people of color may be shared. One African American/European American man described his experience.

There are a lot of hostile people—from a racial perspective—in my town. . . . A lot of times . . . friends . . . don't see me as an outsider, they see me as an insider. There have been times when I'd hear the worst things from my friends, like, "Oh, he's not Black"; "We don't think of you as Black, you're one of us." That's an insult. . . . So I'm in a situation where I am on the inside . . . and the people talk as they normally would, because they don't see me as an outsider. . . . And so I really get to know what people's feelings are in certain situations. . . . Some of these people are my best friends—people who would do anything for me, and in many cases they tend to be the most bigoted individuals that you could ever meet. (Voice 35)

Such racial insensitivity constitutes an important encounter with White racism for Biracial Americans and people of color who have significant relationships with European Americans.

Confronting Colorism

A consequence of White hegemony is colorism among people of color. Colorism implies that people of color evaluate and discriminate among other people of color on the basis of skin tone. Such evaluative standards exist not only among African Americans but also among Latino Americans as well as other peoples of color.[3] On the one hand, light-skinned people may discriminate against darker-skinned people and, on the other, darker people may challenge the racial loyalty of light-skinned people. Biracial Americans often perceive that they experience colorism in their daily lives.

One African American/European American woman recalled that in the Black Student Union at her college, light-skinned women "always were suspect and you went through a process of having to prove" that you were Black.

I was continually suspect. [People thought] that I really was a White person in disguise and I really was out to support White people. . . . In fact, someone once said to me—we were in an argument about people's freedom to interact with other people . . . and issues about loyalty and racism—and she just said, "You just don't understand, because you're White." That's the first time that anyone had accused [me] of that, but . . . tons of people thought that. . . . Certainly I went through the experience of wishing that I was darker. (Voice 41)

A number of project participants voiced the desire to have a darker skin tone so that other people of color would acknowledge their racial identity and not challenge their racial loyalty.

One African American/European American woman offered a sophisticated sociological explanation for colorism.

As the class of people of oppression in the system, it is much easier to direct
your anger, your frustration, your pain towards one another or [toward] people or individuals who share . . . the same power plane than to direct your anger
to much more powerful individuals, and that is why the intraracial conflict . . .
happens so much more often, tears us so much more apart, in fact immobilizes
us from being able to be responsive to the outside racism that has much more
power to dictate our lives. . . . I think the relationships we have to Whites are
very different, because there's a different power dynamic going on and it's not
threatening for Whites to accept you as Latino or to accept you as a Black person to the extent . . . [that] their status as a White individual is continually pro-
tected. (Voice 1)

Based on an assumption of White hegemony, this woman perceives
colorism not only as a weapon against structural equals but as a distrac-
tion from the more important racism imposed by such a hegemonic
structure. Her analysis of the structural sources and implications of
colorism is compelling.

Shattering Racial Stereotypes

Aware of the nuances of the dominant White culture, achieve-
ment-oriented Biracial Americans often adopt a conscious strategy of
shattering racial stereotypes in their encounters with White Americans.
In these encounters, the Biracial person intentionally behaves in a way
that contradicts and calls into question race-based social expectations
with respect to language and performance. Such encounters may occur
in various settings—in the classroom, in the workplace, and in the department store. One African American/European American woman
described how she always sought to excel in school, because, "I believed very strongly that people didn't believe I could do well in school,
because I was Black." Therefore, this woman strove "to achieve in
whatever sphere I was in," so that her high achievement would become
people's stereotype of Blacks' capabilities rather than a negative stereotype of low-achievement. (Voice 41) A man of African American and
Middle-Eastern American parentage reported that he had enjoyed being in sales territories where no other Blacks had been in order to break
"down some of the stereotypes" that his accounts "might have had
about working with African Americans" (Voice 4). A European Ameri-

can/Asian woman who runs a dating service vividly described how she challenges her clients' racial biases:

I ask people when they initially come in for their interview, "Which race would you care to go out with—Caucasian, Black, Middle Eastern, Indian?" And a lot of times I'll say, "Oriental—Asian?" And they'll say, "No." And I'll say, "Well, I'm half-Asian." And the man'll say, "Oh, well, then I'd make an exception!" People have a very warped idea of different races sometimes. And I'll ask about religion and they'll say absolutely no to Jewish—a lot of people even say, "Everything but Jewish." . . . And I'll say, "Well, you know, there are always exceptions; I'm Jewish." (Voice 49)

A European American/African American woman also described how she has always enjoyed challenging people's stereotypical expectations of her as a Black woman, whether in stores or in other settings of daily life. She said, "I enjoy being able to hold conversations with people that don't expect me to be able to" (Voice 11). These examples demonstrate how high-achieving Biracial Americans may seek to disabuse European Americans of their negative stereotypes about people of color.

In addition to such purposive shattering of racial stereotypes, Biracial Americans may unintentionally challenge people's preconceived conceptions of their racial identity and its implications. A number of people described the surprise that people sometimes had when meeting them after first talking to them on the telephone. A legal advocate, a woman of African American and European American parentage, laughingly related such a recent experience.

My clients often will talk to me on the phone before they've met me. A woman did this about two weeks ago. It was really quite funny. I told her she needed to come in so I could look at her papers. . . . and she came down [to my office]. I had finished up with somebody and I walked over. She was the only person in the waiting area and they had called me so I knew it was she. I said, "Oh, hi, Ms. X. How are you?" She said, "Oh, hi." It was all in a split second and you know what she said to me? She said something like, "You're not who I expected" or, "You sound different on the phone." I just chuckled. After she left, I said to the receptionist, "She thought I was White." . . . It happens all the time. This woman was White . . . [but] my African American clients will come out and say, "I thought you were White." And we'll talk about it and then go about our business. (Voice 41)

Shattering racial stereotypes in interpersonal encounters, then, may be intentional or unintentional. Nevertheless, in both situations the Biracial person not only challenges but changes the other person's perceptions of people of color.

Hitherto my analysis has suggested that shattering racial stereotypes in interpersonal encounters leads to enhanced perceptions of people of colors' capabilities. In certain institutional contexts, however, exceeding performance expectations may have negative consequences for the person of color. One woman of African American and European American parentage described her negative experience as an administrator in several academic institutions when she outperformed her supervisors' expectations.

In the field of higher education, people want to hire capable people of color . . . but I think once you get there, there are problems. . . . What happens is that they offer you the job and you take it and . . . the institution . . . has a preconceived view of what your capabilities are. And then I think you ride through the first year and you start to show that your abilities can exceed what their expectations were; and once that starts taking shape, then you start running into problems, because suddenly it becomes clear to the White establishment that you have the ability to far exceed what their highest expectations were and then suddenly you become a threat to this establishment and . . . a power struggle starts to set in. . . . Institutions think that they're ready for [racial integration], but they're really not. (Voice 29)

Exceeding performance expectations, then, can prove problematic for the Biracial American in an institution that cannot adjust to the implications of shattered stereotypes.

While all people of color encounter White culture and racism in the United States, the Biracial American experience is more complex. Biracial Americans with European American parentage are integrally related both to the dominant culture and to other ethnic cultures. Their liminality[4] complicates the meaning and significance of their encounter with White culture. Not only are they betwixt and between customary racial categories but they are both one and the other, with attendant personal identity challenges and choices.

PERSONAL LIFE THEMES

Changing Self Constructs

As I have discussed earlier, not only may Biracial people opt to identify with one of their racial heritages, with both, or with neither in theory, but all three choices are represented among project participants in actuality. (See chapter 3, "Biracial American Identity Choices.") During the course of their lives many have chosen different racial identity labels in response to changing social environments. Moreover, at any given time people may use different racial self-descriptors depending on the social contexts in which they find themselves. Most of these Biracial Americans, then, experience changing self-constructs in their adult lives and many have experienced changes in their primary racial self-identities over time.

Today, many project participants have selected a monoracial identity as their primary racial identity. Almost without exception, this monoracial identity is an identity of color. Other Biracial Americans have chosen an inclusive racial identity embracing all of their racial heritages and some, a raceless identity. Many Biracial Americans identify themselves as "African American" or "Black"; one woman calls herself "Latina," another "Cape Verdean," while others use such inclusive Biracial categories as "Chinese/German American," or "Black and Korean." Others use multiple descriptors, depending on the social context. In different social settings, for example, one man may identify himself as "African American," "Black," or "Biracial."

Although most of these young adult Biracial Americans stated that their current primary racial identity is the one that they have always claimed, many acknowledge having assumed different racial identities in the past. Several have changed from a negative racial identity of "Unknown" or "Other" to either a positive affirmation of an identity of color such as "Black" or to a positive affirmation of both their racial heritages, such as "Chinese/German American." Others have changed from a Biracial identity to a monoracial identity of color or to a positive identification with multiple racial heritages. Still others once claimed a monoracial identity of color and now assert a synonymous cultural identity, such as changing their self-descriptor from "Black" to "African American"; still others have moved from a monoracial identity of color to a raceless identity, such as from "Black" to "Human." Often these changes in primary racial self-descriptors were associated with moving from one community to another, from one school to another, from one peer group to another. In other cases, changing self-constructs were attributed to heightened cultural and political awareness.

The life theme of changing self-constructs pervades the discourse of many young adult Biracial Americans as they reflect on racial identity issues in their lives. One man of African American and Middle-Eastern American parentage noted that as a young child he identified himself as "African American and half White" until he learned more about Middle Eastern culture in high school, when he "became 'African American and Syrian,' not 'African American and White'" (Voice 4). Another very politically conscious man of European American and African American parentage related how he briefly became "Tan" rather than "Black." When this man spent several months in India during his high school years, he decided that he was 'Tan' and that he "had this global affinity with [the] color that the majority of the world is—which is tan. But that didn't work too well, because emotionally I was Black" (Voice 31). Another African American/European American man mused on his positive identity transformation to "Black and White" from "Not White and Not Black," explaining, "And that's what I was; it was the absence of something, not a declaration or an affirmation. But that's reflective of my experience. . . . Culturally I was much more White than I was Black—and that's true to this day" (Voice 14). A woman of Asian and European American parentage said that she preferred to define her racial identity in increasingly descriptive terms as she matured. She stated, "[Today] I identify myself as Chinese/German American. Probably for most of my life I didn't identify myself and then I think for a while, I identified myself as Asian American. The more I go along it just seems to me the more specific the better" (Voice 36).

The fluidity of racial labels claimed at different life stages indicates the arbitrariness of racial constructs in American society, suggesting that for many, racial identity is kaleidoscopic, with racial self-identifications changing in different social contexts and over time.

Engaging in Silent Struggles

Running through many Biracial Americans' reflections on the development of their racial identity is the theme of silent struggle. Many never discussed their feelings about race with anyone as they were growing up; some did not know how their own racial experience differed from their siblings' encounters, because they had never discussed such issues together; others were silent about racial identity issues in adolescence, whereas they had discussed them with their parents earlier in childhood or with friends and parents in adulthood. Some have grappled with their families' denial of their racial identity. In childhood and adolescence, some found the personal conflict engendered by their dual racial heritage too painful to confront. One man recalled that as an adolescent he regarded himself as a raceless individual, while a woman spoke of the continuing "war within myself" that she experiences as an adult.

Another silent struggle that many Biracial Americans confront is fear
of and experience of racial rejection. One person who is phenotypically
European American vividly recalled his boyhood fear of possible rejection should peers or employers learn that his father was African American. Others experienced rejection from relatives as well as
acquaintances. One young woman described how when she was seven
or eight years old, her mother would send her to her room when a certain visitor came to the house; another recalled how her grandmother
told her never to identify herself as her grandchild to the grandmother's
friends. Several mentioned that the racial rejection that they experienced from childhood and adolescent peers had made them less outgo-
ing than they had been in early childhood.

Several young adults recalled situations in which they had failed to
disclose their racial identify for fear of rejection. One man of European
American and African American parentage, for example, stated,

I can recall a couple of incidents that I was embarrassed by later. I don't know
whether my brother went through this, we've never talked about it. Occasionally they would take a census in my high school in our home room. You'd
have thirty or so kids, all of them White, and they would ask demographic
questions like . . ."How many of you are Asian?" No one raises their hand.
"How many of you are African American?" And because everyone else was
White, I can recall trying to duck my head when they would ask the census and
I would not even respond. The teacher would say, "Okay, I didn't think so."
They would completely overlook me, so I think my teachers did not think I was
Black. (Voice 38)

This revealing statement discloses the man's remembered fear of racial
rejection should his racial identity become known by high school peers
and teachers, his guilt at harboring those feelings, and his solitary struggle with the issue, which he never discussed with his younger
brother—neither at the time nor in later years.

Self-censorship on racial issues constitutes another response to fear
of racial rejection and is another form of silent struggle. One woman of
African American and European American parentage, for example, recalled that although she asked her mother about racial issues, she felt
"that my feelings about race" might be "a little bit unorthodox, so I
didn't want to alert anybody to the fact that I might be having different
thoughts, so I didn't want to share them with anybody" (Voice 32).
Rather than risk rejection for unusual racial views, this woman chose to
censor the expression of her ideas.

The Biracial Americans with whom I talked recalled experiences of racial rejection in various forms and at different developmental life stages. For the most part, they have coped independently with these negative experiences. They have waged silent struggles to achieve positive self-identities as Biracial Americans. The theme of silent struggle recurs throughout my interviews with Biracial young adults.

Encountering Color Conundrums

Among the various identifiers of race in American society, none is more salient than skin tone. Skin tone is the visual cue, corroborated by facial features and hair texture, that Americans use to classify one another as African American, European American, Latino American, or Asian American. Biracial Americans, whose skin hues range from very dark to very light, confront several color conundrums.

Since most Americans use only monoracial categories, they classify Biracial Americans as African American, Asian American, or European American on the basis of skin tone. Such categorization may differ from a person's self-identification. One woman of European American and Afro-Latino parentage, who identifies herself as "Latina," vividly describes her own experience with racial labels. "White people think I'm White; Black people, depending where they've been—usually not Hispanic—might think I'm White; and Latinos always claim me—always" (Voice 37). Another woman, who claims her African American, Asian, and Native American heritages, recounted regional differences in the way other Americans identified her: Polynesian on the West Coast, Caribbean on the East Coast. Although skin tone may be the primary identifier of race in America, its validity is highly specious.

Biracial Americans who are very fair skinned may be perceived as European Americans by others but may identify themselves as people of color. Such-fair skinned people may find themselves in situations in which European Americans make racist remarks about people of color and must decide whether or not to reveal their racial affiliations. To do so creates social tension; not to do so means denying a fundamental aspect of themselves. Conversely, dark-skinned Biracial people may confront the same problem with people of color who make racist comments about European Americans.

Lighter skinned Biracial people whose heritage of color is identifiable often perceive that European Americans are more comfortable with them than with darker skinned people of color. One woman of African American and European American parentage stated,

I've never thought that I could consider any color privilege, because I think people clearly line me up as being African American; . . . within that construct, it's easier for White people generally to deal with me, because I'm not that far removed in skin tone, and I recognize that. And that became apparent to me in college and certainly is apparent to me in professional [settings] when people interact with me differently than with a colleague or a friend who's more dark skinned than I am. (Voice 41)

While lighter skinned Biracial Americans often acknowledge the comfort they perceive that European Americans have with them, they also attest that African Americans frequently challenge their African American identity.

Light-skinned people of color confront distinct privileges and problems. If other Americans perceive light-skinned Biracial people to be "White," they experience "White-skin privilege" in public settings—in stores and on streets. The situational nature of White-skin privilege was acknowledged by one woman of European American and Afro-Latino parentage: "I lose my White-skin privilege whenever I'm with my . . . mother's family side or my brother or my mother. . . . I made a choice early on to be very conscious of that and not to pass for White, because I was so close to my mom" (Voice 37). Several project participants thought that as children they received preferential treatment, teachers complimented them on their light complexions, they were treated more kindly than their darker friends, or they had more European American friends than did their darker siblings. At the same time, since most of these light-skinned people identify themselves as people of color, they experience discomfort with white-skin privilege. Several light-skinned project participants expressed the wish that they had darker skin so that both European Americans and Americans of color would readily identify them as persons of color.

In addition, given that most Americans use monoracial categories, other Americans neither consider the reality of a person's Biraciality nor positively acknowledge their Biracial heritage. The darker a Biracial person's skin tone, the more likely they are to be socially recognized and treated as people of color by other Americans. The lighter their skin tone, the more likely they are to be socially recognized either as light-skinned people of color or as European Americans. If Biracial people are thought to be European Americans, they can choose either to assert their status as persons of color or to accept European American status with readily acknowledged social and personal costs.

Experiencing the "Squeeze" of Oppression

As mixed race people, Biracial Americans spoke of having experienced rejection from African Americans, European Americans, Latino Americans, and Asian Americans. Young Biracial Americans bear witness in their discourse to what Maria Root has identified as a "'squeeze' of oppression *as* people of color and *by* people of color." (Root 1992: 5)

The situations in which people recalled experiencing the squeeze of oppression ranged from their school days to their current lives. One woman of African American and Asian parentage remembered, "When I was younger, I felt . . . like an outcast, because I was too light to be Black and I was too dark to be White; I was mistreated by both sides. That's one reason why I always stuck by myself. . . . Now that I'm older . . . I really don't take the time to be bothered with those things, . . . though I do tend to get it—more from Black people than I do from White people now" (Voice 5). Another African American/European American woman recalled,

It was in high school that I had really awful experiences with my friends who were White, which really made me rethink . . . relationships with White people. . . . Equally, in college I had some very hard, painful experiences with African American students. I felt like I got thrown from one side to the other and then found myself sitting in the middle, so I think generally . . . as an adult developing relationships . . . I really do take my time and I'm very cautious. . . . I do have a sense of myself as Sarah and how I interacted with people as a kid and Sarah, and how I interact with people as an adult and I really do feel the difference in that person. And the differences are the product of my experiences around how people treated me based on my race and how that made me have to put up protective mechanisms, because I really wasn't up for getting hurt all the time. . . . An important issue for me around having relationships—particularly with White people—is . . . how willing are they to make an effort—to do their work and to do their own education? Because that's going to make a difference in how willing I am to invest any energy in this relationship. (Voice 41)

As this young woman's statement indicates, the squeeze of oppression from people of color and from European Americans can produce lasting effects on Biracial Americans' orientations toward others.

Although the squeeze of oppression is invariably painful, rejection by people of color is particularly problematic. A woman of African American and European American parentage recalled that in college,

[t]here was a certain somewhat militant fringe of Black students who felt as though you should belong to the Third World Center, you should have Black

roommates, . . . you should hang out with Black people. It just never occurred to me to start thinking like that. . . . Even though I had Black friends there, I didn't make an extra effort to just be around Black people at least ninety percent of the time. . . . [So] I got a reputation for being one of the Black people who wasn't really Black. (Voice 25)

One light-skinned man of European American and African American parentage stated, "I've always wanted to be accepted by the entire population of Black people and have sometimes found that difficult, and that's very painful." (Voice 31) Biracial Americans, then, experience rejection not only by European Americans but by people of color. Since most Biracial Americans identify themselves as people of color, experiencing oppression from people of color with whom they identify is especially wrenching.

Negotiating Cultures

Biracial people are liminal people, betwixt and between customary racial categories. In their liminality they find their greatest source of strength and their greatest liability. Many attribute their ability to move comfortably between cultures to their Biracial heritage. Several people spoke of viewing themselves as "bridges" between cultures and valuing that role, while others talked of moving easily between cultural worlds. One woman of African American and European American parentage noted that she felt she derived special insights from her straddling of two cultures, while an Asian/European American woman said, "I see myself as straddling the fence and having a lot of negotiating skills" (Voice 36). Yet another African American/European American woman maintained that her Biracial heritage made it possible to work with people of vastly different experiences. A man of European American and African American parentage commented, "I can flow into and out of any situation that I've come into with a certain amount of grace. And I think that comes out of just having to be a chameleon to a certain extent in many situations. . . . I think acting comes very naturally to the late twentieth-century middle-class Biracial" (Voice 31). Biracial Americans, then, perceive themselves to be facile cross-cultural navigators and take pride in that role.[5]

Nevertheless, this dual heritage that enables individuals to encounter and move in different cultural milieus is also the source of their feelings of being outsiders; of not belonging to any racial and cultural group. Nearly all Biracial Americans interviewed irrespective of the sources of their Biraciality—African American, Asian American, Latino American—spoke about both aspects of their Biracial experience. Almost without exception, Biracial Americans talked of "not fitting in" or "not belonging" as troublesome aspects of their childhood or adolescence—and sometimes of their adult lives. Several spoke of not fitting into either the European American world or the world of color, or of being too light to be Black and too dark to be White. A number spoke of feeling lonely because they did not belong to a socially recognized racial group.

Claiming a place that establishes a comfortable racial identity with integrity is a major challenge that Biracial Americans confront and variously resolve. Most assume a monoracial public identity of color, some a Biracial identity, and a few, a monoracial European American identity.

The young adults with whom I talked share the common personal experiential life themes of self-construct changes, silent struggles, color conundrums, squeezes of oppression, and cultural negotiations. Irrespective of the different sources of their Biraciality, they share these life themes. While American society may more readily accept Biracial Americans whose heritages include Asian, American Indian, and Latino roots than they do those whose heritages include African American sources, Biracial Americans of all heritages grapple with the same existential life themes as they seek to establish a place in American life.

NOTES

1. See Werner Sollors, *Neither Black Nor White Yet Both: Thematic Explorations of Interracial Literature* (New York: Oxford University Press, 1997), especially 246–284, for an overview of passing in literature and G. Reginald Daniel, "Passers and Pluralists: Subverting the Racial Divide," in Root 1992: 91–107 for a sociocultural analysis of passing. For a recent description of passing in an African American family, see Shirlee Taylor Haizlip, *The Sweeter the Juice* (New York: Simon and Schuster, 1994).

2. See Table XX in Part II for identification of voices.

3. One African-American/European-American woman recalled colorism in the family of a Latino friend. "Latinos have that [color prejudice] just as much. . . . My friend's mother is a great example; her mother is a really black Latina. . . . As children, my friend [and his siblings] never met their mother's mother; [their mother] left the home; she never wanted her children to know her [mother] or meet her—she was so ashamed of her mother. And my friend's nieces—one . . . is fairly light skinned and then he has another who is [darker] about my skin color; . . . his mother treats [them differently; the light-skinned one] is clearly her favorite. . . . Latinos speak about "White La-

tinos" and "Black Latinos" . . . Latinos do the same things that we [Americans] do around color." (Voice 41)

4. The concept of liminal status entered social anthropological discourse through Arnold van Gennep's classic 1907 study, *The Rites of Passage* (Chicago: University of Chicago Press, 1960) and was developed further in twentieth-century anthropological analyses of ritual and status, most notably by Victor Turner. More recently, G. Reginald Daniel has utilized the concept in discussing multiracial identities, as in his essay, "Beyond Black and White," in Root 1992: 333–341.

5. Several social scientists have described the cross-cultural negotiating skills of Biracial Americans, including Teresa K. Williams, "Prism Lives: Identity of Binational Amerasians," in Root 1992: 280–303.

Part II
Biracial American Voices

Part II complements the analysis of part I by presenting project participants' direct responses to inquiries about their remembrances and perspectives as Biracial Americans. Its chapters cluster project participants'
responses to related interview questions. Chapter 6, "Development of
Racial Identities," comprises responses to questions about racial labels
and identity changes over time. Chapter 7 is based on queries relating to
childhood memories of racial issues and experiences. Chapter 8, "Family
Relationships Remembered," pertains to parents and parents' relatives.
Chapter 9, "Assessments of the Biracial American Experience," derives
from questions asking project participants to assess and reflect upon their
experiences as Biracial people. These chapters convey the diversity of
project participants' perspectives and experiences in their own words.
The range and cadence of these young adult Biracial Americans' voices
reveal the heterogeneity of their life experiences, of their orientations toward the world, and of their personalities.

The responding voices in part II were selected for their import. They
are neither all the responses to any given question nor necessarily the full
response to a question of the individual quoted. These responses are ordered to demonstrate the range of response to different questions. While
none of these responses duplicates quotations in part I, they may be read
in reference to analytical sections in part I. To preserve confidentiality,
personal names and, often, place names have been changed within response statements, which have been edited to delete thought-collecting
repetitions of daily discourse.

Table XX
Biracial American Voices

Voice	Gender	Birth Year	Occupation	Racial Self-Descriptor	Father's Racial Identity	Mother's Racial Identity
1	Woman	1969	graduate student	African American	African American	European American
2	Woman	1967	law student	Black	African	European American
3	Woman	1965	receptionist	Dominican	European American	Afro-Latino
4	Man	1964	management consultant	African American	Middle Eastern	African American
5	Woman	1960	accountant/ model	African-Asian American	African American	Asian
6	Woman	1968	saleswoman	African American	African American	European American
7	Woman	1961	accountant	Black	African American	Asian
8	Man	1960	mailhandler	Afro-Asian	African American	Asian
9	Woman	1963	college administrator	Black/ Biracial	African	European American
10	Man	1966	college student	Black	European American	African American
11	Woman	1959	librarian	African American	European American	African American

Table XX (continued)

12	Man	1958	camp director	Italian-Native American-African American	European American	African American-Native American
13	Woman	1962	model	African American/Mixed	African American	European American
14	Man	1965	café manager	Black+White	African American	European American
15	Man	1968	community developer	Other/Mixed	European American	Afro-Caribbean
16	Woman	1966	graduate student	Black	African American	European American
17	Woman	1969	writer	Biracial/African American	African American	European American
18	Man	1966	project manager	Black-Korean	African American	Asian
19	Woman	1959	lawyer	Korean-African American-Native American-European	African American	Asian
20	Man	1965	law student	African American-German	African American	European
21	Man	1961	salesman	Multiracial	Asian Caribbean	Afro-Caribbean
22	Woman	1968	writer	Black	African American	European American
23	Man	1963	account manager	African American-Syrian	African American	Middle Eastern American
24	Woman	1969	graduate student	Human	African American	European American

Table XX (continued)

25	Woman	1965	project manager	Black	African American	European American
26	Man	1965	planning analyst	African American	African American	Asian
27	Woman	1966	medical student	Black	African American	European
28	Woman	1970	graduate student	Biracial/ Black	Afro-Caribbean	European
29	Woman	1963	college administrator	African American	African American	European American
30	Woman	1970	secretary	(none)	Asian	Afro-Caribbean
31	Man	1970	writer	Black	European American	African American
32	Woman	1963	lawyer	Black	African American	European American
33	Man	1961	graduate student	(none)	African American	European American
34	Man	1970	salesman	Black	African	European American
35	Man	1965	college student	Black	African American	European American
36	Woman	1969	writer	Chinese-German American	Asian	European American
37	Woman	1962	lawyer	Latino American	European	Afro-Latino
38	Man	1963	social scientist	African American	European American	African American

Table XX (continued)

39	Woman	1970	photo-grapher	African-Asian American	African American	Asian
40	Woman	1963	home-maker	Other/ Unknown	African American	European American
41	Woman	1966	legal advocate	African American	African American	European American
42	Woman	1970	secretary	White-Black American	African American	European
43	Woman	1969	writer	African American-European American-Native American	European American	African American-Native American
44	Man	1969	teacher	African American	European American	African American
45	Man	1961	artist	Black	European American	African American
46	Woman	1968	adminis-trator	African American	African American	European
47	Man	1962	corrections officer	Other/Black-Korean	African American	Asian
48	Man	1970	college student	Mulatto	African American	European American
49	Woman	1960	saleswoman	(none)	European American	Asian

Responding voices are numbered. One number is identified with one voice throughout parts I and II, enabling readers to trace a voice as it recurs in different chapters. In Table XX, I identify each voice by certain sociological attributes: gender, birth year, occupation, current racial self-descriptor, and birthparents' racial identities. This information allows readers to create a social context for different voices while permiting them to develop their own sociocultural analyses of the implications of these variant Biracial American perspectives.

6

Development of Racial Identities

This chapter presents individual responses to two queries about racial self-identification and its stability and variability over time. The first question asked, "You identified yourself as _____. Have you always identified yourself that way? If not, what other ways have you identified yourself—when and why?" The second question inquired, "What do you consider are important turning points in the development of your racial identity?" Responses to these questions reveal an individual's changing racial self-descriptors over time, social contexts that impose racial labels and produce changes in those labels, and the frequent discrepancy between private and public identities. (See chapter 3 for an analysis of issues discussed in this chapter.)

RACIAL SELF-IDENTIFICATION

[I identify myself as "African American" or "African Irish."] Growing up I thought of myself as mixed. . . . I probably would have said "Black" or I would have said "Well, my mom's White and my dad's Black." So I think that's pretty much how it was up to and through high school. Then in college when I started thinking differently about myself, I think I started to realize that I had to make a choice; I had to decide what I was going to do and I couldn't really just say, "Oh, I'm mixed." That's when I think the shift came of saying "Black" or "African American." Now it depends on the company. (Voice 1)

[I identify myself as "Black"] in the context of writing . . . forms. . . . I haven't reconciled [my internal image] yet. To be honest, I don't really know, because on the one hand, I feel Black and I identify most strongly with Black people in general. . . . I know that I'm Black and I'm White. But I don't even look at it like that, I look at it more like I'm part of my mom and I'm part of my dad; I don't really see them as Black or White. (Voice 2)

[I identify myself as "African American" or] "Black." . . . If people ask me, though, "What are you made of?," I tell them specifically if I think that's what they're asking. If they're asking me how do I identify myself, how do I see myself, what group do I see myself with, I say "African American." I used to say "Black." I think I feel a little more comfortable with "African American," although I don't think "Black" is a terrible term to use; I just like the other one better. . . . I think people shouldn't value or base how they see people . . . on their color; identifying ourselves as a color continues that way of thinking. . . . There's been a lot of positive things about African culture that I learned from interacting with a number of Africans or reading about African things that I'd like to include as part of my identity. (Voice 4)

Well, I have always [identified myself as "Black,"] but early on in my life I fought and fought to be viewed as "Black" and I used to cry, because I was so different. I used to pray, please can I be darker, can my hair be different? I think when you're young, it's so hard not to be just like other people. And I think that I finally accepted that I was different, that it was ok, many many years later. . . . For me, I want to be "Black" . . . but when I think about my racial makeup, I ask myself now why is it that I have to be "Black," that [it] is not fair; I want to be "Black," . . . I've chosen and that's what I want to be. . . . Being "Black" in this country is sort of like pouring curdled milk into something—you know, oops, that's it, you've got to be this one way. And I know there are kids out there that may want to be something else, and I think, well, why can't they be, if that's what they want to be? And so on that level I think about it, but for myself, I identify with Black people and being Black is what I want to be. (Voice 32)

It's always been "African American." I know I have a little Irish on my father's side and there's some Cherokee, but I would never, ever call myself Native American. But I've tried to learn as much as possible about my mother's background, because . . . I'm also very much White, too. . . . It's a weird thing, being half and half. . . . I identify myself as "African American," but there are things I do that aren't typically Black things, or the way I look isn't, but then again I like being different from everybody and anybody, so it doesn't matter. And another thing I don't like, I just don't like that things have to be labeled. Why should certain things be Black and certain things be White? (Voice 6)

I have always identified myself as "Black." There was a time in my life when . . . I was going to say "I'm 'Mixed,'" because, God damn it, that's what I am. I must have been in high school and going through a little bit of an identity crisis. I remember my sister telling me and I was just p.o.ed about it, she said, "If you have an ounce of Black in you, then you're Black." And I said, "Well, that's true, but, Merry, we have this whole other side to who we are. What about that? Don't we want to learn about that too?" (Voice 7)

I think I was "Biracial" for a really long time and then I decided that Black culture needed me more. And that I was and am very, very much "Black." You know, I'm not sure what "Biracial" means. I think that when I became "Black" was when I really realized I was uncomfortable with the term "Biracial." It's also coming full circle. When I first became aware of my Blackness, I really was ashamed about it and I love it now. I needed to do that; I needed to come full circle. (Voice 17)

[I have always identified myself as "Black and Korean."] When I was taking achievement tests growing up, every time they came back with the race column blank, because they wouldn't accept two answers. I would check "Black" and "Asian" or whatever choice I had for both of them, but then when I saw the form, it came back blank. . . . If you don't put down "Black," you're not going to be counted when people do statistics of Black people, so then I started checking "Black." (Voice 18)

[I identify myself as "Afro-Asian."] I never really thought about it, because it never really became clear that I had to have a choice. . . . Well, I came up with ["Afro-Asian"] while I was in the military. Up until the time I went in the military, I didn't know of too many Blacks with an Asian mix, but when I went in the military, I found that it was a common thing. There were a lot of Black kids with Asian mothers. . . . When I went in the Army, I did notice that there was tons of kids that were mixed . . . so then I figured out that that was where the world itself was going to come, to a point where one couldn't identify with one single race. (Voice 8)

I have never identified as "White." I know Biracial people who do and I could never do that. It seems morally wrong to me. People ask me, "You're half and half. Why do you choose to be 'Black?'" And to me that just seems like such an insulting question. [In this society] you don't have a choice. Now maybe if I looked light enough to pass and if I could look at myself in the mirror in the morning, I could say, "Okay, I'm going to choose to be 'White;'" maybe I could justify it. But the way I am it would be absolutely ridiculous. But also, I think—given what Black means in our society and about the stuff that we have to deal with—it has nothing to do with how I feel inside but—politically—with whom I need to be aligned. (Voice 9)

I really didn't want to identify myself as "Black" until the eleventh grade, because I thought that it was an issue that was easier just to push aside and just really have idealistic views. The communities that I was in and the friends I had really saw no colors—which is not really how it was, or the truth. (Voice 10)

I identify myself [as "African American"] not because of what I think but because of what everybody else thinks. And it's easier. You don't write "mulatto" or "half-breed" on a form—those aren't nice words, but it's very descriptive of what I am, because I don't feel like a Black person; I mean I am. It's just being Jewish—I was raised Jewish; I went to temple and that's the way I was raised. . . . Because of the way that I was brought up, Black people look at me like I'm strange, too! When I was at Columbia, I'd walk down the streets in Harlem and they knew I didn't live in Harlem; they knew that I went to Columbia; they knew that there was something different about me. I'm able to speak standard English if nothing else! (Voice 11)

[I was and am culturally White.] But I still did not feel a part of what I was culturally; I never felt safe within the [White] community and I always was conscious of race. It's something I'm constantly aware of. I was telling my dad a while back that if I'm going to the bathroom in a truck stop and I'm sitting there with a bunch of White men, I feel it; I feel like I'm in hostile territory, even though they may not be feeling a single thing about it or thinking one way or the other. It's a sensation I get. (Voice 14)

I went back to Miami in 1990, my mother was very ill and I had to move her from L.A. to Miami and find work that I thought could support us both. I had really been drawing toward education and I had this engineering degree and I felt I had some understanding of different groups. And I thought, geez, I'm always hearing that they need math and science teachers, let me go see. Well, I went to the personnel office of the Dade County public schools; it's the fourth largest school district in the nation and like most school districts it's incredibly overlaid with bureaucracy and red tape. . . . I was told that I couldn't teach on a full-time basis, because they would need to send my transcript off to the state capitol and it might take four months to find out if I had enough math and science to teach seventh graders. That's number one, but number two; on their racial list, they had no "other." . . . I didn't see anything that really fit me. I felt I was a hodgepodge of several [categories], so I created a box that said "other." And a lady came up to me while I was paying them thirty bucks to do my fingerprints and said, "You cannot do this." And I said, "Do what?" She said, "You cannot create your own category." I said, "Well, ma'am, you have nothing that fits me. Can I just not answer the question, would that be the simplest thing? Shall I just leave it blank?" "Well, no; if you don't answer the question, if you don't check a box, we can't put you in the computer and you won't exist." (Voice 15)

I don't consider myself "half White and half Black"; I consider myself "half German and half Black." And that has a lot to do with my mother having made it very important that I get to know the German culture, so I've spent a lot of time there. I've learned the language and the culture. If I couldn't speak German, I probably wouldn't consider myself half German, I would say half White, but since I so closely identify with Germany and all of my family basically is in Germany, I think that I feel an affinity.

From the age of ten or twelve onwards . . . I realized that kids, based on the color of my skin, would make up their minds about me—Black and White. So that's why I said I don't want to be "Black"; I don't want to be "White." Had the Black kids accepted me, I probably would have said I was "Black," but neither group had shit to say.

At the age of ten or twelve I used to get angry that I was Biracial. Thereafter I decided that I wasn't Black, that I wasn't White, that I was John and that was the way I dealt with it; it wasn't a race thing any more. It was the only way that I could feel any sense of ease about the situation and I did feel much better; it helped me for a long time until later. So during the years from the age thirteen or fourteen until maybe twenty or twenty-one even that's how I looked at these things. (Voice 20)

At one time I identified myself as "African American and half White." Because of the pain and experience that my grandparents felt being Syrian and the discrimination, they felt that they almost hid their culture. [In the Pennsylvania city they first lived in,] the Syrians lived in one neighborhood, the few Blacks in another, the Italians, the Polish, the Jews lived in another—very segregated. But because they were light, they didn't have the dark Middle-Eastern features, they almost were passing as White, and so I always assumed that my mom was White. . . . As I learned more about their culture in high school, I became "African American/Syrian" not "African American/White." I knew I always looked different than other people; I don't ever think—even though my behaviors and things I would do may have been similar to what a White person would do—I never thought of myself as being White. . . . I was just who I was, and I gained that strength and pride from my father being such a strong person and my mother instilling a lot of confidence, and through the stories—my father saying, "You've got to be better than somebody who's White doing the same thing. That's reality. You're looked at a little bit differently." That was from his business experience. (Voice 23)

I've never really considered race. I would never consider myself White; but I guess, because of the community in which I grew up—being at times the only one, I've never really had an identity in that manner. Although I guess those incidents at college at least have made me aware of the "Other" check on the form or just leaving it blank. (Voice 22)

I didn't start thinking about being brown and really having a racial identity until I was about twenty-two . . . when I was in California. Until then I really had
not done that and part of the reason it got postponed was when I went to New
York [to college], I came into contact with all sorts of different peoples. . . . In
New York nothing matters. . . . So actually that was an interesting environment, because I didn't feel ostracized at all for being Black. . . . Although when
I was an undergraduate, I was a Martin Luther King, Jr. Scholar, so I had an
all-Black group there, which really didn't amount to all that much. . . . There
were always issues that came up about racism. And that was one of the first
times that I really was exposed to it, but I can remember a [Black] girl . . . my
freshman year saying, "Don't you feel racism in your life?" And me saying,
"No, not at all." And her just thinking I was the biggest loser. . . . And I think
why it was so difficult to start thinking about these issues was, because, if you
think about it, for me to have to think about being brown or Black would have
totally ostracized me from the most important person in my life, who was this
blond-haired, blue-eyed mother that I had. And so I didn't really . . . start delv-
ing into that until I was feeling much more independent. (Voice 24)

I think the only [time I] identified myself as anything other [than "Black"]
must have been right within the past couple of years since I met Betty [my
White birthmother]. And I still consider myself "Black" and I still have these
conversations about, "Well, White folks just do this or that." And Betty even
asked me, "If I had raised you, wouldn't you consider yourself 'White?'" And I
said, "No," without missing a beat, and she was kind of hurt and surprised; she
said, "You wouldn't?" And I said, "I don't look White, that's number one, and
it's just too much the history of this country, if you're any part Black, you are
'Black.' I agree with you, I'm just as much White as I am Black, but you're not
socialized that way." Since I've met her, I do think . . . that . . . her contribution
to what I am should not just be brushed away or become like a footnote. And
then just occasionally, I've thought about things on different forms whether I
should put "Other"; I could never really think of myself as "White." My son,
for example, is very racially mixed and on one form for his daycare provider I
just filled out for U.S. government statistics, they ask what is his ethnic heritage. And I thought, "Well, if they're specifically asking for heritage, I'll check
off his heritage"; there were eight different things to check off and I checked
off six! So I've done that and it's probably something that I never would have
done before.
　　Especially living here in Sea Town, it makes you more Black, because it's
only 1.5% or 1.3% of the population is Black, so it's essentially White. . . . I
know that Jim, [my husband,] is darker than I am, but he doesn't necessarily
look Black. People think he's Indian or maybe he's Hispanic. With me sometimes people know I'm Black, but I've had occasions where they haven't, and it
just cracks me up, and I've had people say, "Well, what are you?" And I'm saying to myself and thinking, "Come on, you have to have had some experience

with people who may not look exactly like you expect a Black person to look; you know there's a wide range out there!" (Voice 25)

["African American"] and "Black"—I use them interchangeably. But I can see the merit in identifying yourself as African to give your race some sort of existence that precedes slavery and because slavery is not a great thing to spring from. . . . I always find it peculiar—Black is literally a color. . . . I mean if we're going to label ourselves. [It's interesting because we're always changing our labels in this society.] It's like Reggie Jackson said; in the fifties he was a "Negro," in the sixties he was "colored," in the seventies he was "Black," in the eighties he was "Afro-American." (Voice 26)

[I don't identify myself racially.] I'm not really into the concept of race . . . partly because I don't think it's accurate. I think that when people are asking about race, they're actually asking a whole set of very different questions. I think that they're asking you very complicated things like, "What class are you?," "What position are you likely to take in a certain political debate?," "What has your experience been?" It's used as a short cut to get a whole lot of information about where the person came from, where the person's going, what kind of life they've had, and it's usually very inaccurate; that's why I avoid the idea. (Voice 33)

TURNING POINTS IN RACIAL IDENTITY DEVELOPMENT

I have always had a strong racial identity. . . . My sense as a kid is that's always been there. I think the piece I've struggled with the most is figuring how not to fall into the traps of the stereotypical expectations of who one should be based on either their race, or their background, or whatever, and how to carve out a self that's whatever you choose to define it. I think that's the continuous challenge of being a Biracial person. . . . Some Biracial people say, "Black is what I am"; it's almost as if there's no side of them that has any component of being of another culture, of another race. I really have tried not to take that route. . . . I think of myself as a Black person; I identify myself as an African American; I don't think of myself as a White person. There are other Biracial people who say, "I'm Black and I'm White, and that's what I am, I'm both of them, don't make me one." That doesn't work into my rationale of it. (Voice 41)

When I was very young, I was challenged by other Black kids, "You're not Black; you're not Black; you can't play with us." I was a timid child, so I befriended the darkest girl in our neighborhood and she fought for me. She said, "Yes, she is Black and if she can't play, I'm not playing." And as I grew older, . . . I became . . . the Blackest person you could ever meet. I wanted to prove to everybody how Black I was. Slang wasn't allowed in my house, so I couldn't go that route, but I could learn the dances and I could be especially chic . . . that happened about middle school. When I started attending high school, I changed completely. I dated a White guy at school and I decided I'm not going to let other people define who I am. I can still be a Black person and pursue my individuality. Then I left and went to a historically Black college and I came back and I hated White people. I broke up with my boyfriend . . . and I went through this complete change. After college, I swung to the middle and decided that I could be a Black person and like other races, and I just came back to normal. I went through three changes. (Voice 32)

Growing up in New York City, . . . I chose a Hispanic identity, but I would say for a long time that I was Puerto Rican. And then my mother is part Puerto Rican, her mother was Puerto Rican, but she was born and raised in the Dominican Republic. There are differences between those two cultures, but growing up in New York City, I thought that if you were Hispanic, you were Puerto Rican. . . . The first summer that I actually went to the Dominican Republic . . . I met all my mother's family, and all of a sudden, I took on a Dominican identity. . . . And I went through a real brief phase where I would say that I was mixed. I think I was in college when I went through a phase where I was denying this, denying that. . . . There are also points in my development where I went through a phase when I felt that people should not intermarry, that everyone should marry their own kind, and it would be so much easier. . . . I never felt one hundred percent comfortable in the Hispanic world. I learned Spanish as a second language. I wasn't raised in a "traditional Hispanic household"; we used English at home. My mother's a nonconformist in a lot of ways, so I wasn't raised with racist ideas, homophobic ideas. . . . So sometimes I didn't really feel comfortable with Latinos . . . then I certainly never felt really welcome in the Jewish tradition. I didn't really know enough about it; I feel that my father really was neglectful in his responsibilities. . . . If you are mixed and have kids, then you should always teach your kids about your culture, whatever it is and whoever you are, so they know you and know your thing equally on both sides. (Voice 37)

Oh, there are so many. I can recall . . . having a guidance counselor or college counselor ask me about my curly hair. I remember one time I wrote an essay. I was about twelve or thirteen. I wrote an essay for school where we were asked to talk about some issue of race or social background. . . . But I wrote in that essay how I would feel if I were from a poor background, how I would feel if I were Black. I wrote a sentence, "If I were Black, I would feel. . . ." My mom saw that. She was pretty upset and she said, "What are you thinking? Obviously. Don't you mean to say, 'Because I am Black, I feel. . . .'" And I realized that I wanted so much to be like the other kids in [my town], and there were no other Black kids, so it was easy to duck my head when they were doing the census count in homeroom and then to write things like, "If I were," to really duck my background. I guess I really was passing. . . . And I realized during that period that no matter what I would do, I was going to be different from the other kids. I don't want to make myself sound as though I were that unique. One of the things that my mother kept trying to express to me as I was growing up was that I was not unique; there were so many other interracial children and my experiences were so similar to other Black kids', yet I knew my experiences were not so similar to other Black kids who were darker; that simply couldn't be. So many of my experiences were based on the fact that I was somewhat ambiguous looking. So I think that experiences like that led me to understand that I was carving out a new identity for myself. . . . I began to realize that . . . unhappy as I was at times [in my home town] that that was transitory and that I would find a better place. I was starting to realize at that time that I was going to be different from the other kids, and—clearly—my mom had been stressing to me that I was a Black American kid with ancestry from a lot of different parts of the world. She didn't stress that as much . . . , because, as she knew, my social identity would have to be based upon my minority status by virtue of this one drop of African ancestry. So I was starting to realize at the time, I'm going to be a different kind of Black American no matter what I do.

One of the things that really solidified my identity for me as I was going to college, . . . applying to schools, your racial identity is thrust upon you. Which box will you check? I was relieved to be able to check "Black," "African American"; to be able to do that and feel some conviction or sense of correctness in that choice. At this time I was sixteen or seventeen. When I went to visit schools . . . , this question again was thrust in my face in that often I went to minority recruitment weekends. . . . As a light-skinned Black kid from suburban upstate New York not having been with large numbers of Black kids in my high school years, going to minority recruitment weekends where kids from urban high schools were attending and darker kids; they shared a culture, a language, and a way of expressing themselves that I had lost since my years in Detroit. That was kind of difficult. This was upon me again and I had to figure out, "Now, where am I going to create my space here? . . . I have to fit in with these people and yet I know I'm different, I don't look like them, I don't act like many of these kids, how can I create my space here?" . . . I felt most comfortable after my visit at Harvard, but a lot of the kids would ask me, "What is your background?" I would tell them, "Well, both my parents were light-skinned Blacks," because I didn't want them to think that I was a Biracial kid. I remember putting on a little bit of an accent . . . and trying to act like an urban Black kid, but I had lost that from Detroit. And so those memories are almost embarrassing, because when I think back on it now, I wish I had been myself, because in fact at a place like Harvard there were so many other kids like me. . . . One of the things that's interesting when you bring in that wide socioeconomic range, especially among Black students, all the Black students try to blend to one common denominator, [the urban denominator]. . . . I tried to be the urban Black kid . . . but then I realized that there are so many other kids here from so many different backgrounds. . . . That was a turning point for me that first year—I really became more comfortable defining my own space. I definitely appreciated my Detroit experience with my grandparents' Southern roots, because that helped me to relate to a lot of kids who had similar experiences, but by the same token having spent time in more suburban communities, I could fit in with some of the White kids. So I could create my own space [in college]. . . . I'm still changing and evolving. (Voice 38)

In my life it would be the exposure [through] busing [to class differences among Blacks] while I was in Connecticut. . . . Blacks were being bused in from other communities . . . the Olatunji concert [at twelve], because it gave me my first real sense of pride in being Black—realizing that there is a subculture within the dominant culture. . . . Another turning point would be moving to California. . . . Coming out here from a predominantly White culture, in time I was able to adjust and to round myself out better to where I wasn't just hanging with Whites and wasn't just hanging with Blacks. I'd always had exposure to White culture . . . and I've seen other Biracial kids just hang with what they were comfortable with, but through athletics and teams, I'd had limited exposure in the East, but it was enough to know that I could become comfortable, because oftentimes in sports, we're working on common goals, so I would have a multiracial group of friends. Davis was another turning point. As a freshman in college, I was up there early to play football and the Equal Opportunity Program [students,] who were mostly Blacks, were up there before school started. I didn't get in through EOP, I was playing football, so I felt out of the loop. Here they had had three weeks with one another . . . so I really had to make a concerted effort to reach out to people. Because when you look at me, . . . I may look Puerto Rican, some people say Hispanic, some Italian; I think I look Black, but I do look like a mixture where my brother looks more Black than I do.

[Another turning point was] through Nabisco; I started out in the Northwest in a territory that never had Blacks in it . . . so I felt good in exposing some of the accounts that I had—breaking down some of the stereotypes they might have had about working with African Americans. . . . Also, being African American, I was a little bit taken aback, because there weren't many of us up there in the corporate arena. We didn't have very many role models that I could look up to. I think in five years I was the only Black in the organization in northern California. . . . I felt good about opening the door for other African Americans or people of color, because there was such a good experience that I had with the company. (Voice 23)

I developed what could be called a sense of race very late in the ballgame. I would say, later high school, and I think the reason for that is that race is a very American concept and both of my parents moved to the United States after age forty and their way of conceptualizing race and ethnicity and difference was a different ballgame entirely, so I think that I came to it very late. When I came to it in high school, I had very little space in which to express any sort of worries about it, any sort of comments about anything remotely bitter about prejudice against non-Whites was definitely taken among my friends as an exaggeration or just as a "isn't this a neat little cause" type of reaction. (Voice 30)

I'm not sure at what point this happened, but at some point—I think all of us who . . . [are] oppressed people go through some kind of process during which they understand what's going on for them. I think I went through a long period of understanding that I had been discriminated against and understanding that I carry this weight of being a Black person. . . . But there was some point when I just claimed my White part as much as I claimed the Black.

There were a few important turning points. The first one was when I no longer felt that I had to apologize for being Black or that I had to hide it or that I couldn't be proud of it. So I went through a mini-militant phase [in high school and college] where all my politics were about oppressed people and racism.

And then there was the point when . . . I couldn't be just with the Black anti-White scene, because that would mean being anti-part of myself and my family. So I had to reconcile what it meant to be Black and White and then try to forge a new Biracial identity, which I did. You know, it's very difficult in the world as it is, because everyone wants you to be one or the other. And so I really had to create a whole political discourse around being Biracial and to talk about what it meant to be able to be a bridge between cultures and races and to have a vision that that is not necessarily grounded in one or the other. And that was a real turning point, when I started to realize that my very body—in that I embody two races—is sort of a very futuristic emblem concept for where I think the world should go. . . . And I think that move was from a very reactive racialized identity into one that was more humanized. . . . So that was also a turning point in my sophomore year in college. (Voice 43)

I think moving away from Boston and living in Tanzania, I became a little bit more comfortable with my White part also. I think I was more ashamed of being White before, because I was in Roxbury [a Black section of the city] and it was all during the sixties and the early seventies with all that Black power stuff. Then when we moved away, I noticed that it was more unique what I was, as opposed to something bad. And when we came back to Bedford [a Boston suburb], I had one up on the White kids, because they couldn't be Black, but I could relate to what they were and I just became a little more comfortable. I think that the really comfortable part of me didn't come until I probably was twenty-four or twenty-five—accepting it all. I would say that I'm African American; if people know enough to push me to find out more, then I will let them know [that I'm Biracial], but it depends who asks me, too. (Voice 13)

I have no recollections up until about the age of seven of thinking about race. A little bit when we moved to Tanzania; I wasn't African, which was far more important—the cultural difference rather than the racial difference. But the attention I got because of my race, and to them I was a little White boy—I had blond, straight hair at that time—was curiosity, there was nothing hostile about it, nothing inferior/superior about it. . . . Bedford was the beginning. Well, I was an extrovert for sure prior to that—very much a leader in any kind of social group organized in terms of playing games or anything like that, I was always one of the most vocal and active participants. I had no problems with strangers. And when I moved to Bedford, I became an introvert rather quickly. I think most of it came around, certainly, racial slurs and around girls and around sports. People calling me "nigger" and "half breed" and things like that—starting to be good at sports and ways of putting me down in the fifth and sixth grades. (Voice 14)

I'd say in high school [when] I considered myself Dominican. . . . In grammar school if you asked me what I was, I would say whatever served me; I would say "My father's Jewish," and leave it at that. And now to this day . . . I always say "Dominican," and then if they press further, I'll say, "My father's Jewish," and they'll go, "Oh, ok, that explains it." [I began to affirm my Dominican heritage] because I grew up in a household where everyone was very political and very aware, so I just started associating with all the injustices that Hispanics get, and Blacks. . . . I always felt that my teachers treated me differently; they didn't expect as much of me as they did of the other students, and I always felt that that had something to do with my mother being a dark woman. (Voice 3)

High school, dating, marriage, and job. In high school there was a White boy I dated who called me up and said that he couldn't date me any more, because his parents found out I was half Black. There was an incident with a Black boy. In my high school I was a cheerleader; I was very vocal and out there and kind of wild; I was the big enigma of the whole high school from both sides. [This Black] boy used to follow me around the high school; there was an incident of him spitting at me, because he thought I was scoffing him because he was Black, but it was just because he was bothering me. . . . All the Black boys thought that I was God's greatest gift to the race, because I was Black but I was White and that was a very big thing. If you dated me, . . . there were White guys who thought it was a wild thing to do—in a kind of rebellious way, because I looked White but was darkly exotic. It was very troubling to me, because I just wanted to be White, but I never quite was. And college was kind of bizarre, because there were groups of White males who were from the Boston area . . . that were very racist; that would, in the middle of a party, come out with things like, "Isn't she a nigger?" and stuff like that. The first time that I had real blatant racism. . . . It was weird, females weren't the same way, except Black women were really [hostile]. In high school and college, a lot of hostility. (Voice 40)

I really think that Zimbabwe [at thirteen] was a turning point in my life. Before thirteen or certainly in elementary school, certainly the vast majority of my friends were probably White; going into middle school, I had two good African American friends but still a number of White friends. Then we went to Zimbabwe for two years, and then I came back and things changed. . . . When I came back, I was in high school and things changed. . . . My friends became more African American than White.

Then going off to college was definitely a turning point. I went to Johns Hopkins, which is predominantly White, but it's also very conservative and not at all conducive to fostering ones identity as an African American.

Then also I think my going to South Africa . . . in 1989 . . . I was in the University of Cape Town. . . . I was a little surprised, but that experience was really educational and I say that because my major was international relations and I'm even now planning on going back to graduate school to do political science. So South Africa—the whole country, the whole climate was an educational classroom for me. . . . It's a difficult society to just socialize in. If I were just going there to live, I would have a difficult time fitting in. . . . I found UCT to be much more liberal than Johns Hopkins; I was much more inspired by my professors and what we were studying and what we were learning than I was by any of my classes at Johns Hopkins. And these were White professors. . . . It's a predominantly White institution.

[Was it a comfortable place to be?] Not really, because your first instinct—the group of people that you really have most in common with are actually White South Africans, because they really idolize American culture. And they speak your language, and they're the ones that have traveled outside of South Africa and have had similar experiences to what you have had. Unlike in Zimbabwe, I at least did not come into contact with a substantial Black middle class and so most of the Blacks that I came into contact with were very political, they wanted to speak their own language when socializing, which did make one feel left out at times, so I had to overcome that. And they're coming from a very different background than I am. Then the other racial group, the so-called "Coloured"—although if you solely looked at appearances, that is the group I would fit into most easily; again it wasn't a really easy fit there either. So it was difficult. . . . You had to reach out your hand first, because they're not—so they're friendly but not so friendly as to reach out a hand to you. And [they're] quick to judge. (Voice 46)

After ninth grade I couldn't stand living in this [White suburban] community and I told my parents that we just had to move. So we moved to Philadelphia and that was another shock, because at that point I was plunged into Black society. I went to a school that was evenly mixed; it was a magnet school; it was equally mixed between Black, White, and Asian students. At the same time there was the expectation because of how I looked, I should think and behave and speak and wear certain clothes and all of those kinds of things which I didn't do, because how would I do that? I grew up with a few Black friends before I moved to Philadelphia, and so that was very hard, very depressing, and very difficult, because here I was thinking I was going to some kind of Shangri-La where people would finally accept me and it was the opposite. I was rejected and I had been rejected in the other place, too. . . . So I ended up basically hanging out with people who essentially were not trying to fit in at all. I hung out with—some of them were White, some of them were Black; all of them dressed strange; they liked strange music—like New Wave and things like that. . . . I just decided to stop dealing with it at that point. And then when I came to college, I began to have a more positive sense of myself in terms of being Black. Of course, I had the same problems that I had in high school, which were that I don't speak like a Black person and I don't have the same experiences as Black Americans and so it was difficult, but I managed to have a small group of friends to talk about things with and so it was better, and I managed to figure out how to speak the way Black Americans speak. . . . I feel most comfortable with West Indians, just because they don't have this heavy load of race on them. . . . Coming to college allowed me to have more of a positive racial identity, but at the same time it allowed me to see more of the inequalities and things in the curriculum. . . .

I really don't want to live in this country any more. . . . . Race relations in this country are a hopeless cause and I'm not really willing to devote my life to solving the problems here. . . . I haven't really found a place for myself besides the Caribbean where I feel comfortable. I can operate in both worlds, but what am I going to do when my White friends start asking about my hair or when they say that affirmative action is wrong, and what am I going to say when my Black friends say that they think that White people are the devil? . . . It's a matter of belonging everywhere and nowhere at the same time. (Voice 28)

The time in early adolescence, looking at myself in relation to the kids from the METCO [Metropolitan Council for Educational Opportunity] [busing] program. I think another major time would have been in college, struggling with the issue of being in a setting with a lot of ignorant folks and my naïveté going into it, thinking . . . it should be okay yet not realizing that these folks really had no exposure, and feeling a total outsider in this setting. Fortunately, because of people like [my African American friends] creating support networks and through lots of talk and discussion, moving from being very angry at the institution and angry at the people in the community through a period of feeling, "[M]aybe I can do something to help educate these people so this situation does not continue." Making the turning point just at the point where I was about ready to transfer. I remember talking to my mother a lot about that at that point. . . . It was discussion with my mother and with people at college in that support network [that] made that change, which took a huge weight off my shoulders and gave me a different lens for looking at this issue of race and my relationship to this predominantly White setting, which I'd have to continue surviving in and living in any way. It was nice to no longer constantly feel so angry; so that was a very big turning point for me.

I always remember thinking that I'd marry someone White, because my comfort level was just much more at ease with White males. I think a lot of that was just from my background. And then I think through my relationship with crazy Walter Stevens, as crazy as he was, I suddenly found that there were Black males who had an intellect and were bright and interesting to be with and fun to be with, because I really had this very condescending view of a lot of Black males who just want to have fun, and they're not very serious and they're not very bright; it was very negative, other than my relatives, my brother and father. So that relationship really changed my view to realize that I could marry someone White or Black. And that was a very interesting turning point, because I was sure that I would marry someone who was White and who had no issue about being in an interracial relationship. (Voice 29)

I'd say moving to Seattle was one, even though I didn't like it at the time and I didn't understand it. [I denied my Blackness,] and I really, really hurt myself. And another turning point was when I went to college. Those two years, the only thing they were good for is learning about myself, my African American background, the confidence; . . . that was a big help. . . . And even living in San Francisco now, . . . I'm getting more comfortable with myself. I have a hard time being very, very light; I fight it a lot but I think this past year I seem to have really calmed down on that aspect. . . . There are still problems. I live right in the middle of a traditionally Black neighborhood and its projects and Black people all around. (Voice 6)

I'm not sure there are turning points as much as places where people force thinking about race upon you. When I was applying to colleges, . . . [my] school was a very small private school but they hadn't sent anyone anywhere impressive, ever. So in my class of seventeen, a friend of mine and I were the only two to get into Ivy League schools; it was a first in the school's seventy-five year history. So it was a big deal. When I took the SAT and filled out applications, I had a mentor in high school who actually went to Harvard—he himself was half-Cuban and half-Chinese. He mentioned to me once, "Indira, I hope you start checking all those little boxes for race." Being very mean, I said, "Well, no, I'm not going to check any of them." And he said, "If you don't, I'm going to sit at that desk and check them for you." I didn't [check the little boxes]. I was inconsistent—I think on the applications I didn't and on the SAT I did. I definitely either checked all that I thought applied or checked none.

In college . . . I had my first encounter with what you might call Black culture and, "Why are you not fitting in?" and "Why are you not trying?" I don't know if that was a turning point, but it was definitely an awareness. I became a lot more skilled at when to hang and when not to and how to explain my gaps in knowledge, which weren't the class gaps that most ethnic Black Americans thought they were; it wasn't the fact that I went to a private school as much as the fact that I didn't have American parents. To me there was a definite awareness when I was in college rather than a turning point.

And to some extent writing a thesis on identity and ideas of mixed race was a kind of turning point. It allowed me to do a lot of thinking and see what other people's thoughts were. That, I think, was very important, too. (Voice 30)

And a turning point would be in high school when I started identifying with other half-breed kids and you knew that you could fit in with them. I wouldn't hesitate to ask someone if they were mixed or if they were Black or White, because I am. I did not feel that I was invading; usually they would be willing to talk—someone who was Japanese and Black or Black and White. I'd say, "Hey, what are you mixed with?" That was in high school, probably when I was in tenth grade, about fifteen, when I started realizing that you were not going to fit with the Koreans or the Whites. . . . One of the earliest girls that I liked was Japanese and Black, so I started gravitating toward other people who were Biracial. (Voice 47)

Probably starting in the working world after high school, getting a little better sense of the way people actually behave—getting away from what you learn in a progressive school. Moving away from that experience and my mother's upbringing and her consciousness of race and mine, and her attempt to instill a consciousness of race in me. Getting out in the working world and seeing how much more gray—how much less black and white—how much more gray the world is, that was a turning point.

My mother is an Afrophile. She always was taking me to cultural things, you know, the Black museum. . . . She always tried to get a sense of African and African American culture instilled in me. And it never took in me as much as she wanted.

[In the world of work] I found a lot more racism that was used rather than felt. Racism that was a rhetorical strategy . . . held by the late seventies New Yorkers that I was dealing with. Though I was dealing with regular people. It wasn't that my junior high school and high school experiences had been strife-free just because the kids were of upper middle-class and upper-class parents, professional, not just for that reason, but that was a somewhat different world from what my mother grew up in. (Voice 33)

My second year in college, a lot of things happened. I went to college about three months after my father died so I was in a haze, although I didn't really realize it at the time. . . . Most of my friends were just the people who lived in my suite or who lived on my hall, which is to say mostly White people. . . . So for the first couple of years I was basically doing the same kinds of things that I had done in high school and not really thinking about who my friends were and what it meant to be Black in a larger way. . . . I became increasingly unhappy and I just realized that I wasn't happy with who I was any more—that I didn't like the fact that all my friends were White; I didn't like the fact that I knew Black people thought of me as someone who thought of themselves as White and didn't really know who I was. So all that stuff came together for me and I just started thinking more about who I was or who I wanted to be. . . . After that, I worked at the NAACP, so it went from there. . . . Then I went to South Africa two years later after I graduated from college and that really changed me a lot as well. . . . Going there . . . was the first time that I felt a connection to a community. . . . Going there was really amazing for me, because not only did I have a sense of communal practices that had gone on for centuries but there was a group of people who immediately took me in and listened to what I thought about various things. Because there're so may people there who are "coloured," it wasn't a new thing for people to meet someone who was of mixed race.

Growing up I didn't know anyone else who was Biracial. [When] I got to college, there were a lot more people who were Biracial, but . . . you couldn't really have discussions with them about identity, because everyone was really busy. . . . A couple of my close friends from college actually were Biracial, and it was great talking to them. . . . But there were other Biracial people there who had really decided that they could not even think about what it meant to be Biracial in terms of their politics. You'd hear them saying things like, "Oh, White people do this and that." For me, I know my mother didn't think that stuff. So it always made me wonder how they had grown up. (Voice 1)

College [was] the first time I'd ever had contact with a considerable African population. But at the same time, I accepted some alienation from Blacks themselves, for the simple reason that the way I dress and the way I speak . . . I don't necessarily articulate in an inner-city slang, so when the brothers hear me talk, they say, "Whoa, wait a minute." I would suffer the same—or maybe sometimes to a greater extent—prejudice from Blacks, because for all intents and purposes I have lived in White society. My speech, my mannerisms, and the way I dress don't contrast to theirs [i.e., Whites] as much as they contrast to inner-city kids. So when they hear me talk or they talk to me, they prejudge and drop me away, so the McNair Program is the first time that I've really been able to get into it. . . . I was on a leave of absence, because I couldn't afford school. I came in the summer and got in the [McNair] program. . . . That was the first time I had ever had a Black teacher and then I got a feeling of negritude, defining myself for myself and not accepting somebody else's definition of me. . . . It's completely revolutionized my attitude towards school;

it's made me reevaluate my potential. My academic situation has improved considerably as a result. (Voice 35)

There are several turning points. The first one was my first year in college, when my mother for the first time was really concerned that the people I spent a lot of time with were mostly White. She wondered why that was. I got really angry, because I felt that she didn't get to know the people, she only cared that they were White. . . . It made me introspective but it encouraged me to change my patterns at that point. And the second point was junior year. I spent the first semester in London and I found it to be incredibly international—an incredibly good experience. And living side by side with so many races, coexisting in a healthy fashion, versus America. . . . The third turning point I'm still in the midst of. I started dating a woman in my junior year, who looks very much like me; most people think she's my sister. . . . I didn't find out until I met her parents that she was White. . . . We ended up dating for about three and a half years. . . . That made me very introspective, because I started to think about life choices as far as getting married. I really thought, "Is it fair for me to bring into the world children who will be multiracial themselves and be perceived by society as mixed?," and also whether I could handle it from a social perspective.

As an adolescent, a lot of the time I wanted to be White. It was easier in the community I was in. . . . If things didn't go right, the reason why . . . was because I wasn't White. Now I'm very proud of [my Biracial heritage]—very proud that I have the opportunity to not only deal with the White community, because I have the tools to do that, because of my background; I am able to deal with the Black community because of the way I look and experience. I've had a very mixed experience on both sides; I'm a versatile person. . . . From a religious standpoint, I've had a chance to go to church, . . . also I had a bar mitzvah. . . . I'm not an organized religious person, but I feel very lucky to have had [these experiences]. (Voice 44)

The first major one that I can think of was when I was a junior in college and I spent a semester in Chicago in something called the "urban studies program." . . . There was a feminist philosopher and that was the first time I had ever been introduced to the idea of race, gender, class, and social constructions. She definitely changed my life. . . . Finally, someone is telling me something that really matters to me. . . . After I got back from there, I went to Taiwan to study Chinese and I did some writing there for the summer and then I came back and became really active with the Asian group on campus and also with a lot of women's studies things, so that was a big turning point.

Just after graduating from college I moved to Oakland. I think that's the first time in my life that I lived in a diverse setting. (Voice 36)

[In college] I moved in with a high school buddy who happened to be Caucasian, but for all intents and purposes had what you would consider a typically

Black racial experience—he just loved everything that was Black: he loved to play basketball, dated only Black women, loved Black music. And so moving in with him and just seeing how enamored he was with the whole culture and showing everything that was positive about being Black, which was very different from what you see in the media and everything in mainstream society. It took him to show me all the things that were good. . . . He also had a great deal of admiration for me; he thought the world of me, and I convinced him to go to school after high school. . . . I told him that in a lot of ways he gave me great racial pride, because I found out what was good [about] being Black through him.

[Another important turning point] was meeting my wife. I'd dated every race. Still it surprised everyone that the person I ended up being serious with was Black. At the time of meeting her, that wasn't important, but today it's really important for me, because of that fundamental connection that we have—just some of the background and the understanding. While she's Biracial from a racial standpoint, she was raised in an all-Black home and all-Black environment. That was another turning point for me, because now I was saying that I'm without a doubt a Black American, which is kind of bad, because I don't know if it diminishes my mother's contribution to my whole existence. But I just don't know anything about the Japanese culture; I don't think that it's a culture that necessarily embraces me, either. (Voice 26)

Even though I grew up in a diverse way and knowing about different cultures, I didn't really experience race until the Howard Beach incident occurred. My view was that race wasn't really something in my world. . . . And then again, mainly when I went away to college—obviously I don't look Biracial—people would say things, thinking . . . only White people [are present] so they wouldn't offend anyone, and they would say things. [How did you handle that?] Most of the time . . . I just didn't bother; it wasn't important enough to me to make an issue out of it, and then some—I never have ever not wanted to say that I was Biracial; then they'd be shocked and then they'd say, "That's great." But I sometimes think, "What if my skin were darker, they wouldn't think it was so great." . . . I think people think it's great when I tell them I'm Biracial. They say, "Oh, that's great"; they're not prejudiced. But I think the fact that I don't look [Biracial] is . . . sort of comforting. I think there might be different reactions [if I were darker]. . . . People always think I'm Italian. [They ask,] "Are you Italian?" "No, I'm not Italian." I remember being in the dining hall [at college] and meeting a friend; he said, "What are you?" And he kept guessing, guessing, guessing. Then I said, "You have to think really hard." Then when I told him, he said, "Oh." But I've never had a reaction that was a problem with me . . . but then again, I think that it has a lot to do with the fact of the way I look. (Voice 42)

Just recently [I experienced an important turning point]. I think maybe I was naïve really—thinking that you can get what you want just by working hard and

doing whatever it takes. Right now I'm in construction, and I was racially harassed—attacked at a station by a station owner on a job site. And then there was
a lawsuit. My company is all White—everybody there is all White; they had no
idea what to do. They were trying to support me, but they don't know how, and
then they were trying to feel it. But I was called names—"nigger," "jigaboo,"
"Kunta Kinte." I was like, "Wait a sec, you don't understand, I paid my dues—I
went to college, I graduated, it was hard work. And now you're trying to tell me
that I'm just a piece of shit." If I was younger, like four years ago, I probably
would have sent that guy to the hospital. But now I'm older, I'm married, I have
two kids. So I thought about that and I was like, "It's just words, if I hurt this
guy like I want to, then I'm going to get in trouble." That's a turning
point—the first time being called "nigger." . . . This just happened recently; I
was a project manager and I had four superintendents working for me who were
all White, but I was put in that position. I started as a superintendent and I
moved up, and I'm running a job, and I've run a bunch of jobs, and then this
happens. Then I was just telling some people, "Yeah, he killed my American
dream." I thought that you could go about, do what you were doing, get where
you wanted, but I mean there's always people like that. (Voice 18)

Age twenty-two to twenty-four—I moved to California after school and came
into my own in a lot of ways, because I was away from my family, which I think
was really important. . . . Well, I really realized that my life was a lot different
than my mother's. . . . One of the reasons it was different was because I didn't
look like her and that I had a lot of very different experiences because of my
skin color. And I began to think more about what I felt about life and what sort
of values I wanted to have for myself. And so I started thinking about issues of
race and gender and her feelings that she had shared with me on these issues. . . .
And now my family—all these many years later—would say that they totally
ill-prepared me for being a Brown person. We never talked about the fact that I
didn't look like any of them. . . . We just never talked about color. And I think it
was very inappropriate of them to never talk to me about it. I think part of [it]
though, too, is that there's a lot of tension and bad feeling toward my father, a
Black man, so I think that would have brought all that back for my mother. So
she just tended to avoid the whole conversation. (Voice 24)

COMMENT

The responses of these Biracial young adults to questions about racial self-identification and its variability over time disclose the societal
constraints on claiming a Biracial identity for the 1960s-born generation. While certain individuals have chosen to specify their biraciality
more exactly, others have chosen to identify with their heritage of
color, perhaps selecting a different moniker now than in the past. Until

the 2000 census, however, American society refused to permit Biracial Americans to identify themselves other than monoracially. This societal constraint operates not only at the systemic level but at the interpersonal level, as several respondents make clear.

Racial identities may change over time. Changing communities—whether moving to a new neighborhood, visiting another country, or entering college—often evolves into a turning point in the development of a person's racial identity. A racial confrontation with a peer or coworker can also create a new awareness of racial identity. Most people recall experiencing at least one turning point in their racial identity development; a few remember multiple turning points, as I discuss in the chapter, "Biracial American Identity Choices."

7

Childhood Memories of Race

This chapter contains responses to three questions that draw upon childhood memories of race. The first question—also the initial interview question—asked, "What is your first memory of race as a social identity?" (See chapter 3 for a discussion of this topic.) The second question inquired, "While you were growing up, with whom did you share your feelings about race?" The third question queried, "How do you think that your experiences of race differed from those of your siblings, and why?" (See chapter 2 for a discussion of these topics.) Within each set of responses, I have grouped similar responses. The responses to the first question on first memories of race, for example, are ordered from those of individuals who remember always having an awareness of racial identity to those who do not recall such reflections until adolescence.

FIRST MEMORIES OF RACE AND IDENTITY

I don't have any sense of not being "Black" or not being "African American." . . . One of the things about being in our home is you know you're different, because you see the reality of two race groups in your home. It's not so much that you're different, but you know that there's a White world and there are White people and there are Black people and you know that you exist within that. So I don't have a memory of being like, "aha, this is who I am." I think more of my memories are around friends being confused or inquisitive about my parents—why was my dad so dark? . . . And I think that the other thing that just sticks with me is really a sense of when my family moved to the suburbs, my father being really clear about having a real strong racial identity and being proud of being Black and not allowing people to make us feel that we were lacking and really advocating us fighting people who were willing to call us racial slurs and not willing to demean us. And I think in some ways that was really important . . . saying, "You have a right to stand up for yourself and . . . I will support you if you do." . . . Another thing is, I'm the youngest of three Black kids going through a White [school] system and I think in some ways my older siblings probably bore the brunt of certain experiences more than I did, because by the time I got there everybody had had the exposure. . . . They paved the road for me around certain things. (Voice 41)

Growing up in New York City, I was always around different kinds of people. I think I always knew that there were different kinds of people in the world and because my mother is very much a brown person, I just visually saw it. I didn't know its significance. I understood she was different from me.

I do remember rejecting Judaism at some point, but I never knew what happened. And my mom tells me that it was basically that I said something to my grandmother, my father's mother. I must have been five or six, when you say things like, "Oh, I'm Jewish too," and she said, "Oh, no, you're not; you're not Jewish." And my mother said that I never discussed it again. I must have been so hurt. I don't have a memory of that. But I do remember closing down. . . . That's my first time that I must have made conscious decisions about what I was and what I wasn't.

I think it wasn't until a lot later that I understood the significance of the fact that my mother was a brown person and I wasn't. And that was from being places with her and being treated differently or noticing that things were being said to her that I thought were nasty or rude, and that was [in] high school. (Voice 37)

Well, when I was perhaps three or four, I remember being on a plane with my mother and having someone come up and say, "Oh, what a cute little boy!" and fawning over me. . . . My hair was short and curly. . . . I didn't have the traditional markers; I had two earrings, so I don't know how she did that. Yes, she wasn't looking; she was looking at my brownness. And I remember feeling a self-consciousness about the way she was looking at me that I associate now with the kind of uncomfortableness I feel when I'm being racially interrogated or racially mutilated. (Voice 16)

Going to kindergarten, just based on how you looked at five years old went a long way to determining whether you were popular or in the in-crowd. I remember people reacted to people just based on physical features. . . . This was 1970. If you were fair-skinned and had "good hair" and it was long, then you were somebody whom people gravitated toward, even if you were five years old. And I remember my sister, who is fairer than I am, running home, because kids were calling her "Whitey." It was an all-Black neighborhood, an all-Black school. And she wanted her hair cut short into an Afro and she had at the same time very curly but soft hair and she would, I guess, have an Afro, but it was more a "mass of curls" hair style. So my mother did finally cut it. . . . But I do remember those sorts of feelings and noticing that we were Black. It was an all-Black school with Black teachers and a few White teachers, but noticing that how you looked made a difference. And if you looked a certain way and it was more White than Black, then you were more popular or desired as a friend or thought to be smarter—people just gravitated to you more. (Voice 25)

When I was four, my mom had come to school at some point. The kids found out that she was White. I was asked by a kid in the bathroom once whether or not I had a line down the middle of me that separated out the black and the white. That was probably the first memory that I have. (Voice 1)

I recall my mother talking about our mixed ancestry, starting at maybe age five or six. . . . It was always discussed as, "This is our blood," and "Here's your grandfather and here's what his blood was." But the implications of this . . . wasn't made at that age. I wasn't told our family's White Bahamian or we're mixed-blood Bahamian or such and such. . . . I can't talk about my early conceptions or my evolving sense of racial identity without talking about the Cubans in Miami. Because I came from the Bahamas with a thick Caribbean accent in English and yet I was fair skinned and I spoke no Spanish. If you're fair skinned and you speak no Spanish and you go to an all-Latino school, the kids will call you and the teachers will tend to think of you as Anglo. So I was called "el gringo" or "el Americano." Well, I was el Americano in the sense that my citizenship is American, I was born in the States and I clearly wasn't Latino. (Voice 15)

When I was a little girl, I was the only Black child in my house; I had [White half-] siblings. And they would call me "nigger," when I was little. I was adopted when I was about six. I was living at home with my mom and my siblings. At first I didn't know what it meant, but I thought it must be bad. When I found out what it meant, I don't think I felt persecuted; I was pretty young, but I knew that I was different; I was different in my house. (Voice 32)

When I moved from New York to my grandmother's house in Massachusetts, I remember my first day in elementary school, because I had come in contact with a completely different population than when I was in New York; they were all White kids. . . . I knew I was different but not as much as they knew I was different. So I found myself in a confrontational situation—in many cases with people who were older and larger than I was. So I had to learn to become very verbally adept in order to deal with them. . . . I used to get chased home every day. . . . And there was nothing I could do, because my father had left and I had no man in my family. . . . When I was in New York, I was with half African American and Caucasian kids, so it wasn't as much of a cultural shock as it was when I came to the suburbs. (Voice 35)

When I was six, I went to a private Catholic school. I think being one of two Black kids in the class is my first memory, even though there's no direct incident. . . . But I think I remember being alone. There were other subtle things about race [around] . . . nine or ten. My best friend Penny was Black and I remember her not being invited every year to one girl's party, who happened to be our friend as well, a very good friend. And she kept telling me that her mother selected who she was going to invite and I think when we were twelve, we determined . . . it was because Penny was Black and for me it was okay. . . . She was darker and I was [lighter and] a good-example kid in the class. (Voice 39)

Moving to Bedford when I was seven, I think there was myself and one other Black student in the class. And that other student was [bused] from Boston. That was the first time that I think I noticed the difference between Black and White in terms of color. I thought it was odd that there weren't other Black students who lived in Bedford and the very few others lived in Boston. The teachers would get us confused, they thought I should go on the bus at the end of the day to go back to Boston. I always had to remind them. (Voice 29)

When I was about seven years old in the second grade in a really small private girls' school, . . . Jenny, my best friend, and I were playing; we were reenacting "The Hardy Boys." And Marie, another girl, wanted to play with us; Jenny and I did not want to play with her. So we made up some excuse—we told her, "You can't play a certain character in the whole series, because you are skinny and this character was ridiculously fat." Her response to me was, "Well, you can't play one of the two Hardy boys, because you are Black." And that's my first memory of race. I burst out into tears; I was that kind of a child. I just cried and cried and cried. (Voice 30)

I think it was in fourth grade and the Sonny and Cher song "Half Breed" came out. The school I went to . . . went from the fourth to the eighth grade. It was at the beginning of the year, because I'd never been around bigger kids and some of the seventh and eighth graders were taunting me about the song. I remember going home from school. My parents were divorced and I got off the bus at my father's house, which was very unusual, and confronted him and demanded to know . . . about being half-breed. I told him how the kids called me "half and half" and my big question was—was there going to be a part of me that was going to turn black and a part of me that was going to turn white? It was very, very serious. My father and stepmother laughed like they thought it was hilarious. I was wondering if it was going to be my upper torso and bottom torso and hoping that that was what it would be, because I thought it wouldn't be too strange if that was what it was. Well, you know, to this day I hate that song. (Voice 40)

It must go back to about third grade. Sometimes, because my parents were interracial, there were kids saying, "Oh, she thinks she's cute, because she's light-skinned and she's got nice hair." So I started coming to this realization that we're different. (Voice 7)

It's public school in the fifth grade. . . . My mother put me in a bilingual class and I remember really hating White people. . . . I thought that they were really inferior. . . . My father showed up for a performance I had and I completely pretended I didn't know who he was, because I was so embarrassed. [The kids said,] "Oh, my God, your father's White! Oh, my God!" I said, "That's not my father." (Voice 3)

My parents settled in a small country town in Massachusetts. At the time there weren't any Black families in the area at all; we were the first ones. . . . I started having problems in the second grade. Kids would call us names and I can remember fighting then. . . . We had to fight from then on up to eighth grade and then one or two more times in high school. But [in] the town we were raised in we were the first and the only Black family up until the tenth grade in high school. (Voice 8)

I probably was about eight years old and we went to the Lowland School in Roxbury; it just became an issue when people realized that my mother was White. They called me "White girl." I was very upset. When we lived in Roxbury at that time, I was very embarrassed about being outside with my mother; I didn't like that at all. I was fine in any other setting. (Voice 13)

I remember not thinking much about [racial identity], feeling very free and a really joyful kid. Then when I was in the fifth grade around ten, my best friend and I were standing outside at recess and we were talking with the teacher who was monitoring recess. She was telling my friend how pretty she was. She's very Anglo looking with dark and very beautiful eyes and pale skin. And she said to my friend, "You know, you're very, very beautiful." And then she looked over at me and said, "And you're very pretty too, for a Black girl." So that's when I started thinking, there's something wrong with this picture. . . . I guess what it was for me before was just having really pretty skin and then it became dirty and bad, because it was just not at all what I was surrounded by. (Voice 17)

Actually I never started thinking about race until I moved to Nigeria and I had to be around fourteen or fifteen. When I think about it now—and I do think about this a lot, because I think when you grow up in an interracial household, you struggle with this racial identity thing; I know it's been true for myself and also the different friends that I have that are also Biracial. And I'm not quite sure what made me start thinking about it. I think what was key was that when I moved to Africa [for two years], I spent a lot of time going through the West Coast and started looking around. You were like, wait a second, how come things are so underdeveloped here [in Africa] and how come we have so much over here [in the United States]? . . . Somehow it seems to boil down to race. (Voice 2)

REMEMBERING SHARING FEELINGS ABOUT RACE

You know, that makes me cry a little bit, because I don't think I really shared them with anybody. I wish I could have. Let me see. I could talk about them with my mother but on a very political and so abstract level. There was so much I couldn't explain to people who couldn't feel it the same way, and so I didn't really talk about it that much with anyone. (Voice 43)

This is the first time that I've ever talked [about my feelings about my Biracial identity]. . . . I was constantly asked about it; "What are you?" In high school I really hit as hard a time as I'm having now. I used to share that with my foster mother, so I couldn't voice what it was about being different, because everyone was struggling with that. (Voice 40)

I talked to my mom a lot; I grew up around a lot of community activist types and a lot of my mom's friends . . . were older than me, but they were still young people. In particular, one of my mother's good friends was half-Black, half-Puerto Rican and she was really helpful in my being able to talk to someone who was mixed. . . . Growing up, I would talk to her a lot about how I felt around race, about where I belonged. I think she was probably one of the people whom I spoke to the most and the one who made me realize that it was okay for me to choose. . . . She was really good at making me realize that yes, you have to choose or a choice will be made for you. (Voice 37)

When I was in grammar school, my friend Penny and myself were best friends and we'd get together and stuff about that would always come out—noticing little things. . . . In high school my friend Elizabeth and my friend Judith, we had running jokes, race jokes, especially from "Welcome Back, Kotter." My friend Judith, I always called her "Jewrican" and so we'd joke about why she was going to this party, because she was Jewish and then the Puerto Rican side comes out and she's loud—just different jokes like that—just silly based-on-stereotype jokes. (Voice 39)

I didn't start talking about race until [at eleven] I met my birthmother who is also White, but who is very, very sophisticated about culture. The man she was with at the time was Puerto Rican and her two sons are Biracial. So I started discussing race with her. (Voice 17)

[My mother] didn't understand how much I was going through. I kept it all in and I was a very introverted child. I remember at a certain age, I think I was around eleven, I would come home and I would cry and pray to God; I would blast out God and my family indirectly—"Why did you? Why couldn't you just let me be White or Black, because then I'd know?" And I think a lot of that was a re-action to what the kids were doing to me, and letting that affect me. (Voice 20)

I was incredibly sheltered, because from an early age, I went into the Black niche and just stayed there and was very comfortable and never questioned anything. I think that when I'm with a whole bunch of Black people, people can tell or know that I'm half Black and so I was easily accepted into all groups or at social events. So I really did not have any questions about racial things for a very long time; I don't remember discussing anything. (Voice 27)

Well, in adolescence—nobody; I didn't talk about [my feelings about race]. I don't remember talking about it with anyone. . . . But in college it was very much college friends who were African American women and people like [the Director of Admissions]. It didn't necessarily have to be a person of color, but it definitely needed to be someone whom I felt close to and who could under-stand the issues. (Voice 29)

Through jokes I shared with my friends. . . . In sixth grade everyone in our class . . . we started playing "race tag" on the jungle gym. Well, I guess sociologists would find it interesting, but everyone else would find it disgusting. We called each other racial epithets. . . . That was in elementary school. In high school I never really had any candid conversation. It was like I was Black with Black people and I was Black with White people, but I was able—I knew exactly what their world was and that was a part of my world. So I came across to them, probably, as the Black guy who grew up in the all-White neighborhood. (Voice 31)

[I shared my feelings about race with] both my mother and brother. But I think it was difficult with my mother. . . . She has very strong opinions about almost anything. . . . She wanted us to be very clear that we are "African Americans" and that we were not to try to pass or to dismiss our identity. . . . For that I am grate-ful, because I've been able to really understand the importance of that for just my general perspective in my work and in my relationships with people. . . . It was difficult, though, to talk to her about my experiences. I don't think she really understood what it was like to be a fair-skinned Black person. . . . So it was very difficult to talk with her about this kind of thing. My brother and I could talk about it; I think my brother was less sensitive to some of the issues that would confront us; he was off in his own world some of the time. (Voice 38)

SIBLINGS' RACIAL EXPERIENCES

I don't really know [what my siblings' experiences were]. . . . My sister seemed to me to be more rebellious and more political than me. But it's funny, she and I always seemed to have Black friends and Hispanic friends. . . . My brother, I couldn't even tell you. (Voice 3)

It was definitely different, because the world treated me differently. [My sister,] to other people, "looked White"; she could pass for White and I couldn't. I don't think that it made it harder or easier for either of us, because she seems to have a really hard time in a way that I don't. . . . When I was growing up, kids teased me more, because I don't think that kids even noticed what she was and also she was really quiet, shy—the kind of a girl that people don't feel they need to bother, and I was more loud.

   Now, . . . both of us are concerned about learning about Chinese culture and being part of it and feeling good about it. When I see an Asian person, I see myself in them and I feel connected in a certain way. And she feels she doesn't have that [sense of connection] with either side. She says "Well, none of them identify with me." So in a way, she's having a hard time with [her identity] now. (Voice 36)

Well, I had the curly hair and I felt badly for my brother, because I could visibly let it be known that I was Black by just growing out my hair. And if I had my Afro, people would realize that I can't be White. They weren't sure what I was a lot of the time. And I think for my brother, a lot of people just didn't know what he was and a lot of people may have assumed he was White. . . . You have to have a certain amount of experience to realize that light-skinned Blacks are around. A lot of White people don't see light-skinned Blacks or Blacks at all for that matter." (Voice 45)

Well, [my adoptive White siblings] were never called names; they were the right color. And they really sincerely, earnestly tried to understand what that was for me and were very protective about it, but just couldn't know really; they had different problems, different issues, different friends; they couldn't understand my real need to be accepted. (Voice 17)

Well, my [adopted] brother's "White," so he experienced race from the opposite perspective than I would. He had to deal with his thoughts about Black people. . . . We [talked about] the issue—not really deep conversations about it, because it was clear to me that he understood what was going on. He actually turned out to be very interested in African American history, he minored in it in college and he's now studying African history in graduate school. . . . [My adopted sister is "African American."] She had a real hard time, because she didn't really come to terms in her teenage years with the fact that our parents were her real parents. . . . It turns out she eventually got in contact with the people who had given her up. . . . She ended up having a lot of problems with her birth parents and at the same time she really tried to alienate our parents, because she couldn't deal with the fact of having two [sets of] parents. . . . She had a lot of negative things happen to her and I just don't know which ones are race-motivated and which ones are just [because] she put herself in situations, or she had bad luck. (Voice 23)

Well, my brother went to a private boys' Catholic school and I think he had a much harder time. I think he got a lot of peer pressure and our communication broke down once he went to high school. . . . Then we also were competing against each other. There were lots of times when he stressed more of his Cuban American side, because my grandmother is Cuban American . . . she's Afro-Cuban. . . . I just think also that going to an all-boys' school, he was the object of peer pressure and he had such low self-esteem. . . . So I don't know what his perspective was when he was growing up. (Voice 39)

My sister was always darker than I was, especially when she was growing up, because in the summer in Chicago, she would get really dark. . . . She's really light now but she was always much darker, so people either though she was Puerto Rican or what have you. My mother told me once that she was on an "el" train with her and this White woman stared at her with hatred, because I think she's easily recognizable as being Black . . . and this is a major thing with me—good or bad, guilt or no guilt—I just am not that easily recognizable as being Black. . . . I've had things happen to me—I've been beat up, I've been spit on; it's weird, in Chicago I was recognized as being Black but in Seattle not at all. I don't really know what happened to [my sister] in Seattle. (Voice 6)

Although we all consider ourselves Black, I think my sister and brothers really . . . hold strong to the notion that you have a strike against you and you have to rise above your nationality, because people are going to try to hold you down. . . . I just really believe that people are people and so they've accused me of a lot of things, especially because I'm married to a White man. They've accused me of a lot of things—that I don't like Black men . . . and that's just not the case; I just don't look at the world that way. (Voice 7)

[My brother] looks White and his experience was totally the opposite of mine. . . . I also think that I identified more with being Black than my brother did. Just because his skin color is different, he would have to explain why he was Black, as opposed to explaining that he was something else. (Voice 13)

My brother pretty much identified himself as Black, so he mingled among Black Americans. My sister and myself, we had the same type of friends, which were young Jewish kids as well as young Black kids that were middle class, as opposed to my brother . . . who just went one way altogether. I think it was mainly because he was the lightest one of all of us and he wanted to identify himself as Black; if he went around more, he felt that he had an identity crisis instead of feeling that he was considered to be an "oreo," so he picked up more of the urban Black culture as opposed to my sister and myself—we tried to broaden our horizons. (Voice 21)

I had a tendency to be extremely quiet; I also had longer hair than they had, and I'm the fairest of all the children. And I had more of a problem. Because I was quiet, people used to think that meant I thought I was better than they were, where my brother and sister were more like the buddy-buddy hang-out type. People used to want to fight me all the time; I used to have people who would tie my hair up in knots [in elementary school]. . . . The people that I hung out with in high school were considered the smart group of kids and they all stayed out of trouble. I was the different one [among my siblings]. (Voice 5)

Well, being the oldest, I had no role models to look at. I think my younger brother, who's a year younger than me, had a very, very similar experience; my youngest brother who's now a sophomore at Yale had a similar experience as far as finding it easy with his White friends, but he knew a much wider variety of people. . . . I think the culture by the time he got to high school was more in tune, because of the music that was out then—Black culture—hip hop. (Voice 44)

My [adoptive] sister is also Biracial. I didn't know that [I was Biracial] until I was probably in freshman year in high school, my parents hadn't told me. I knew I was adopted but they didn't tell me I was Biracial. And from that point on, I really thought about it. . . . And my sister didn't want to talk about being adopted at all and certainly didn't want to talk about being Biracial. And even today—she's married to a White guy, actually—and . . . they've talked about what they would raise their children as, because he's White and she's half White. And he actually brought up to her that biologically speaking they're more White than Black, and her response was, "Well, what are you talking about? Both my parents are Black." And he said, "Janice, your parents are Black, that's true, but biologically speaking that's not true." She said, "Well, I've totally adopted their racial identity." And she's closed mouth about being adopted. (Voice 25)

My [Catholic high school] experience definitely set me apart. It did broaden my mind and it just broadened my experience. . . . During high school I didn't identify with Black people as much as I do today, because I didn't hang out with them as much. I didn't necessarily think that Black social concerns necessarily had to be my concerns as well; clearly they still don't, but I'm far more interested. So in high school I wasn't exactly sure that I was African American or just Black or if I was half Black and half Japanese. I think a lot had to do with the circle of friends that I hung out with. (Voice 26)

I think there were differences because of our genders and personalities. My older sister had some more blatant experiences around race than I did. [One boy] called her "nigger." Nobody in my recollection ever made a racial slur [at me]. I think all of us dealt with . . . people wanting to touch our hair, people not knowing who your mother was, because they were looking for a person who was Black and they couldn't understand why you kept pointing to this White woman who was standing there. . . . I think all of us had that experience.

My older sister and I had very different experiences around dating. I dated basically not at all in Concord, I always dated at camp. I dated not at all in Concord; what I ultimately learned was that [that] was based on the fact that I was Black and nothing else. . . . My older sister didn't have that experience, . . . but she dated from eighth grade through twelfth grade, she had a constant relationship. So that was a very different experience and, I think, informs her self-confidence around those kinds of issues.

And I think my sister and I both experienced and continue to experience . . . [similar] experiences around being very intelligent, assertive women of color and continually confronting people who really have problems with that, and consequently having to try to figure our how to manage relationships and interactions with people. So we had differences and some similarities.

My older brother—I don't know diddly in a lot of respects what his experience was or might have been. . . . He made some conscious decisions about his academic performance. I always did well in school and expected myself to do well in school. I wonder if one of the things my brother struggled with was the expectation that Black men don't do well academically. . . . He's incredibly intelligent, but . . . he at some point made a decision . . . about not performing well academically, and not from not being able to do it. I remember once hearing somebody talking on the tape recorder and then realizing it was my brother and being shocked, because the level of discourse was such that I didn't even think he would engage in and that's when I knew he's just playing this game. He was just playing a game and [when he got to college, he changed that]. (Voice 41)

At the same time that I was put into private school, my sister was put into private school; she was three years younger. So we approached it differently and then we were different ages—I was fourteen and she was eleven, and we have different personalities. . . . Our approach was totally different and she accepted what she found around her; I rejected it. She went through a process where she tried to assimilate the culture and be more accepting. . . . We would have radio wars at home. She would want to listen to the rock station and I would want to listen to the disco station. . . . Early on I identified myself as Latina and my sister would always say, "I'm mixed." . . . She always made it clear, whereas unless you probed and asked me, I would not tell you that my father was White.

My brother was a lot younger. . . . He was born when I was fourteen. First of all, he isn't mixed; he's got a different father. He's a full "Hispanic" and he's very dark. He looks very "Hispanic." He's [experienced] direct racism, had direct racist experiences, and he's been beat on. In one of his boarding schools, they wrote "spick" with shaving cream. So he's had the [experience of] direct, direct racism. (Voice 37)

I think in a lot of situations it was a little easier for me to overcome issues, especially in high school, because I was a male. I played sports and . . . I was always like the centerpiece in terms of people always looked up to me, people came to me, so it was okay for me to have Black and White friends without much of a hassle. . . . [People didn't say,] "Oh, you're selling out, because you're not hanging out with all Blacks." . . . I was in the in-crowd in that respect, because I won't limit myself to that, but I was well-respected throughout the high school and I knew a lot of people and I was friendly with almost everybody. (Voice 34)

I don't think mine differed from my sister's too much, but I think I'm the one who passes more easily for White; my brother had a couple of experiences—a lot younger than I ever did—where he became aware of race. I don't even know if he remembers but I think he's got a little more kinky hair than I do and he also tans a different tone—actually we all tan different tones. He tans the brownest, I go kind of gold color. . . . You can tell he's more mixed, more easily.

We were camping once in upstate New York; . . . we were in the campground and there's the path with the bath shower unit down the road. For some reason I went with my mother in the car . . . but my brother walked on ahead and when we got there, he looked kind of bothered. He had walked past a campsite and there'd been a whole bunch of young kids, a bit older than he, and they had called him "nigger" and he was a bit upset. When I walked back with him the next time, nobody said anything. (Voice 27)

COMMENT

The childhood memories in this chapter illustrate the silent struggles that many young adult Biracial Americans experienced as they sought to establish meaningful racial identities for themselves. Many people do not recall discussing their feelings about race with anyone in their formative years, whereas others do remember talking with their mothers or joking with friends about racial matters. Similarly, although most respondents have perceptions of how their experiences of race differed from that of their siblings, relatively few had discussed these issues with their brothers and sisters. Often, perceived experiential differences among siblings related to birth order or to color issues as well as to personality. It is noteworthy that siblings who participated in the project shared similar perceptions of their experiences with race, whether or not they had discussed these perceptions with one another.

More often than not, respondents' first memories of race as a social identity center around a negative experience in early childhood. That experience may be based on peer conflict or challenge, or on a respected adult's subtle rejection or stereotyping. These experiences frequently led to self-doubt and ambivalence about racial self-identity. In thinking about their own families in the future, many respondents intend to be more open with their children about racial encounters and feelings than they remember their parents being.

8

Family Relationships Remembered

This chapter compiles responses to two questions, "While you were growing up, what was your relationship with your parents?" and "While you were growing up, what was your relationship with your parents' families?" (See chapter 2 for a discussion of these topics.) The responses to these two questions disclose the diverse familial experiences among these young adult Biracial American respondents. Some respondents characterize their perceptions of the unchanging nature of their relationships with their parents, while others approach their relationships longitudinally. Some recall very close relationships with their parents' relatives, while others never interacted with them.

REMEMBERED RELATIONSHIPS WITH PARENTS

There were some specific things, I think, regarding race that were important independent of a good relationship that I had with both my parents. . . mainly surrounding my father. Ostensibly I was White. So I grew up feeling like I had a stigma but [one] that was to be discovered at some later point, not in the beginning. So hanging over most anything I did—hanging over parents' nights or soccer games where my parents may come to a game, any social group that I became part of—hanging over all of that was, "What will they think about me when they realize that I'm not White?" That was a constant fear that I had. And I think one of the main reasons it happened was because my father was kind of absent. And if he had just been there and been obvious and prominent within those circles and sports community things, I wouldn't have felt that so much, because it would have been obvious. . . . I can just remember thinking about that a lot and worrying. I wasn't worrying about my mom; I was always worrying about my father—and what kind of rejection that would entail—until I graduated from high school.

Another thing that I regret about my family . . . is that we didn't talk enough about race. My sense is that we had the impression that we know race is not important—that it doesn't matter. At least that was the sense. I actually think that it does matter a lot, but that ultimately it doesn't and in the ideal it doesn't and I do agree with that. And we are an ideal family and a racially mixed family, and, therefore, everything is okay; it's not and it wasn't, because of where we were and regardless of whether or not we were an ideal family, we weren't in an ideal environment. I don't recall ever having a real discussion with my father about my racial identity—that's just appalling to me that that never happened. And that's just really lax, as far as parental responsibilities are concerned, especially in an environment that was particularly hostile—obviously not overtly hostile in the way that certain environments are, but as a kid it was not a comfortable place. And so to the extent that . . . we really did not address issues that were bound to come up, regardless of how hunky dory things were at home. (Voice 14)

We had a really good relationship. My father was a little more distant; I tended to be more clinging toward my mother. . . . My mom and I are still very close, but my father and I have a tendency at times to be closer than my mother and I. I think it's because I'm older and my mom has been always a "do as I say, not as I do" person, while my father has always been straightforward. Whether or not he might hurt you, he lives by his decisions, while my mother can tend to be a little more wishy-washy. (Voice 5)

My mother was the one who enforced all the rules. . . . She was very into education; it was a love-hate relationship. I remember lots of fights with my mother—practicing the piano with her telling me to sit there until I got it right. . . . When I talk to my other friends, we always say, "Asian mothers." . . . Everyone thinks that my mother is the very polite Japanese woman, but you've never seen her when she's angry. . . . And she always had these goals for us. . . . While I was in school, if I ever got in trouble, luckily the principal never said, "I'm going to go get your mother," because that just would have been it. So a lot of things are kept from my mother; even now a lot of things are kept from my mother. . . . And my father is different. . . . I'm trying to do an oral history of my family. Listening to him tell stories about being six and World War II and all those things is great, but in a way he's very closed in a repressed way. So that's how I view him. . . . This always happens, but you hear these things and think, if I knew that then, it would have helped me growing up. (Voice 39)

Because of the professional goals of my parents—my mother, especially, was traveling quite a bit—I also was raised until I was fourteen by a woman who was also my mother's nanny when she was young. And she lived with us most of the year. I see her as just as formative a person in my life as my mother and father, if not more. . . . When I was young until I went away to school, I always thought my parents were very strict, in fact, a little bit unfair. But I realize that they were very moralistic and they just wanted to the best for us as far as instilling values. I always had a very good relationship with them, but again because they weren't around a whole lot, I wouldn't say that we were an emotionally close family. I always enjoy seeing them and I always care very much about them, but we're not a very tight family in the way that some other families are. I had a good relationship with them, but I think that I did not talk as much to them [while I was growing up] as I do now. I definitely came to appreciate them much much more as I got to the second half of college and worked through issues that I needed to work through. (Voice 44)

[While I was growing up,] we moved every four years. My dad was in EEOC [Equal Employment Opportunity Commission] and he worked for various companies . . . I think that moving around created a bond within the family. We became close; our ties became strong, and that was one thing that was constant throughout all those moves.

They always taught me that you don't select people because of the color of their skin but because of who they are. My dad would say, "You have common interests with people not because they're Black, not because they're White, but because of who they are. You may have something in common with some Blacks and with some Whites and with some Asians; it's not because of the color of their skin, it's because of who they are and what they're all about." So I learned that at a young age. (Voice 23)

Well, complicated by lots of other things besides race, like the fact that my father had cancer for most of the time I was growing up . . . I was close to both of them. I probably fought more with my mother and saw my father as a more parental figure than I did my mom. She was more like a friend in a lot of ways. (Voice 1)

I feel a lot of things. I think initially, as a child, I saw my parents not only as disciplinarians but the ones who gave guidance and structure in my life.

I think moving into my young adolescence, it became a more complicated relationship for me, because of my own identity—trying to grapple with—was I Black? Was I White? What did it mean coming from a mixed parentage? I was really struggling internally with that identity from what I saw on the outside that supposedly was being defined in my world as being Black. And that was primarily through METCO students through the school. . . . I would say that seventh and eighth grade was another really difficult time, because that was a time when there were larger numbers of African American students predominantly from families in the Boston area; they acted very differently from me either through language or through mannerisms or through what they did in their families. And they had either single parentage with their mothers or both of their parents were Black. . . . Somehow I saw them as defining what Black was and that suddenly because I had mixed parentage maybe I wasn't absolutely Black; then what was I? And so it was an incredibly difficult time trying to grapple with, what was that all about and what did that mean in relationship to myself and then in relationship to how people perceived me, because I was confused as to what that was. And my social circle really was mixed—predominantly in Bedford my friends were all White, yet because I played athletics, I really was able to move between both worlds. And athletics was that link that allowed me to move. I don't know if the difficulty also was because I was in more advanced classes than a lot of the other Black students. . . . So I think in relationship to my parents it was difficult, because I couldn't figure out what that all meant; sometimes it felt embarrassing to come from a mixed parentage. . . . It was a sense of embarrassment, a sense of not knowing what I was about or who I was and not knowing how to talk about it. I couldn't find a comfortable way in which to say, "I just don't know who I am."

Then moving into high school [I had] more of a comfort level with myself and feeling that I didn't have to define myself either way and that maybe it was okay to say that I was from a mixed parentage. The more that I was able to verbally say that and tell people about that, the more comfort I felt about it. So that if my mother came to a game and someone said, "Oh, is that your mom?," I'd say, "Yeah, that's my mom." And that gave me much more comfort . . . and then realizing that people weren't walking away or treating me differently because I came from a mixed parentage.

And then I think in college, that's really where for me the issue of identity became really solidified, because I just had this yearning to learn more about my African American heritage and also my White heritage and wanted to figure out how I was going to define myself in those two worlds. And I think through my relationship with a number of African American women in school, I really delved into learning more about my African American womanhood. And that really solidified my comfort level with who I was and what I was about and that ended up giving me a sense of pride in coming from this mixed parentage. . . . So I guess my relationships with my mother and father in college very much changed again. I could talk about the issues; I remember talking with my mother more about the issue of identity then, but in adolescence I know I really didn't have the language or the comfort level to talk about it [with her]. (Voice 29)

One of the things I really learned [from my parents] is the ability for cultures to come together. That there really is the capacity for cultures to interact and be supported. I think in my family's house—and I became more conscious of this when I went off to college, because I wondered why it was so hard to be in an all-White environment [at college] when I had been in one all my life. I think what I've learned about that was there wasn't any place [at college] where I could go and be reaffirmed. When I grew up in Concord, I always had that place; I went *home*. The affirmation in the home was not only parental support or support from siblings but it was the ostensible things that I could see. It was that there was African and African American art and there was European [art]; all kinds of [art] together and fitted in and it fit well; nothing had a sense of being out of place. That it all worked; it was all part of the picture and that was really important. That was a really important thing that we had throughout—you walked in; it wasn't in an eclectic sense that something's here or [there], but there really was a merger of cultures.

And I think that my mother as a White person who was really committed to knowing and learning about and understanding other cultures is a really important thing. The fact that she is an anthropologist speaks to the way in which being Biracial in my family is a different experience from being Biracial in other families, because I think the set of learning and respecting and understanding cultures my mother brings into it—it's part of who she is at an intellectual level and at a personal level—I think that we certainly got that. The fact that she knows more about African cultures than a lot of people of color flies in the face of people's [stereotypes]. . . . I do think for me my mother and father served at some level in developing that part of me that's really very resistant to making broad blanket statements, because I've always thought that my mother as an individual and my mother and father as a couple have always held out that there are exceptions to every stereotypical rule. So that that characteristic of myself that is resistant to being boxed in or resistant to people making broad labels, I think that the origin to that is from our family and particularly my parents' relationship and the nature of it. I often think of them as extreme opposites in a number of ways and am amazed how they came together and the longevity of their relationship. It certainly sent messages to me as a child that were really important.

So I do see my mother as much more primary for me; my father certainly was there and there was no question about him being really committed to the family. I do think my mother was much more the person who dealt with the hard things and also dealt with the good things. My mother certainly was the disciplinarian and my father certainly was the one we could get—we knew when my mother went away and we wanted to stay out late, we were set. If we needed a buck or something, he was the person to go to, because we could milk him at any time. (Voice 41)

I lived with both of my parents until they got divorced at the age of ten. My parents tugged at me to decide—they each wanted me to live with them. In the end I decided to live with my mom. I continued to have contact with my dad but definitely not a whole lot. . . . My dad was very strict; he grew up in the

South in Mississippi. . . . He was very authoritarian, but he was a very good man—he never smoked, he never drank, he didn't fool around with other women, he worked very hard, he had a good job, but at the same time he was just very, very strict, and he didn't do a lot of things that were just fun. My mom is a high school teacher and she wasn't, at times, well; she didn't spend much time at home in the evenings and she had her own problems because of the divorce. I as an only child had no one to really talk to, so when I discovered running, I threw myself into it and I became the best. And that's when I discovered self-worth. I discovered the whole idea of what it is to be persevering, to be dedicated, to be respected because you're good at this, to be able to be good at something. (Voice 20)

I lived with my [maternal] grandmother and my brother; . . . and then my mother would come home and we would spend the weekend with my mother. . . . The relationship with my father was pretty much nonexistent. . . . There was a stretch of twelve or thirteen years when I hadn't seen him. . . . My grandmother was the nurturer in our family. (Voice 35)

My relationship with my mother has always been pretty close; it became less close in adolescence. . . . We have different personalities, but I remain a fan of hers and I admire her greatly. And my relationship with my father—I've never met him. We have corresponded; I remember writing him once or twice when I was about twelve years old. . . . I have not had any contact with him since that time; it's been about eighteen years since we last corresponded. (Voice 38)

I remember [my relationship] with my biological mother as being troubled, with my father I remember it as being fascinating, and with my foster mother I remember it being intense. Troubled with my mother, because we were a White family living in a predominantly Black public housing situation and it was a dysfunctional family and there were a lot of problems that that brought. My father was fascinating, because he lived not far away in a middle-class Black neighborhood. He had a house, a yard, a pool, and he was cultured—the weekend warrior dad—and we did a lot of opera, art, theatre, dance, and music, so it was very fascinating. And my foster mother was a woman who had been married three times—to a Mexican, an Irish man, and a Black, so she was pretty wild; she was a radical do-gooder and a very intense household with family therapy and confrontational meetings and this, that, and the other thing. (Voice 40)

With my mother it was difficult at the beginning. I always thought she was real cool; I remember thinking that kind of terminology, not thinking, "I love her so much." I was really thinking how cool she was, because she was so different from other mothers. . . . I had a really hard time; there were times I couldn't stand her. I would say that before high school it was very turbulent always . . .

and then after high school it all changed; I got along with her much better. A lot of it, she said, actually happened when I went to see my dad when I was thirteen. I visited him in New York. Before then I was really wild and crazy and then after that I just calmed down. . . . Then again at the same time all this is going on, she was really different from any of the mothers, she was so cool, I was always proud of her. . . . My father, on the other hand, I didn't have a relationship [with him]. When he came around, I knew he'd buy me stuff, that was pretty much it. I was scared of him growing up, [because] he had a temper . . . if you did something wrong, you got your butt whipped. . . . I was always the one getting into trouble and I was afraid of him. (Voice 6)

I was very mad at my mother for a long time, because of her not even wanting to know anything about Blackness or what that meant about me. . . . I remember coming home once when I was about nineteen and I said that it was very hard being Black. And she said, "Oh, you're not Black. You're just pretending to be. . . . You're my daughter; you're outside of race. I tried to raise you outside of class and outside of race." I know that I was born out of very heady idealistic times; I do think they believed that they were creating a new social order and defying the constraints of their middle-class parents. (Voice 16)

I'm in this [hostile university] environment where I feel it's not the warm soothing environment that you get if you're White, and I tell my mother this. I beat my mother up about race. . . . It's not as though she deserves it because she's White, but damn it, if she's my mother and she married a Black man, she'd best know what's going on in my life and she needs to know about these things. She says I'm very hard on her. But society is very hard on me and if she wants to be close to me—and she's my best friend—if she wants to be close to me, then she has to understand these things. I tell her, when you go to the store, people don't follow you around as though you're going to steal something. When I am with my mother, I look so much like her, . . . Black Americans can see that we're related. White people, all they see is race—they look at you and they see race, race, race; they don't see a person, they just see race—Black, Black, Black. So they can look at two people who look the same except one of them has skin that's slightly darker and they'll say, "Can I help you, Miss?" I'm standing next to her, I'm talking to her; this happens all the time. . . . It's just all these things that pile up, it's so irritating, it drives me crazy. It's very few people that I'll go through the education process that I've put my mother through, because I don't think that most people are worth it. (Voice 28)

My relationship with my father was strained throughout, because they were divorced; there was a distance there, it was a distant relationship; there was a lot of strain as a result of the animosities that developed between my mother and father. . . . My relationship with my mother was very good; she taught us never to look at people for their race but to always look at the character and let that be how we judge or value people within our lives. . . . She taught that everyone was equal and every one was the same. I think because of that—she was Japanese raising her kids in a Black neighborhood . . . for the majority of time, people felt that sense of acceptance and responsibility, so we really did not have a lot of friction with the people around us. (Voice 7)

My brother and I became a unit. My brother and I have a support system. Mom was doing what she thought was right for us, which often conflicted with what we wanted. . . . The more distance that I put between myself and my mom, our relationship really sweetened. . . . Even though I think I'm well loved, I think that everyone [in my extended family] recognizes that I don't see things the way everybody else does. My mom has most difficulties getting me to understand the world the way she wants me to understand it. . . . And my mom has accepted it and I think now she even cherishes that. . . . She still worries about me, simply because I'm more vulnerable; she considers me very vulnerable, simply because I'm not of the guarded nature she is. (Voice 45)

REMEMBERED RELATIONSHIPS WITH PARENTS' FAMILIES

I basically had no contact with my mother's family at all. I really didn't know anything much about them. . . . My mother always said that she had moved away, and she didn't really know them, and I think also she probably wasn't sure how they would take the whole situation, so I really didn't have any contact with them. My father's family—I had contact with his brothers and sisters, but not really the extended family, because there was a lot of tension on my father's side, too, about the marriage and my mom. So there was . . . a rocky relationship, I would say. (Voice 1)

The only person I know in my father's family is my father. And the only people I know in my [maternal] grandmother's family . . . is my grandmother. (Voice 35)

My dad's family . . . are all in Nigeria, so I saw them intermittently . . . until I was about twenty. . . . But my mother's family—when I was younger, I spent an inordinate amount of time with my grandparents and, also, she has five brothers and sisters and we spent a lot of time with them. (Voice 2)

I didn't really see my mother's mother too much, because she lived in the Dominican Republic. But when I did, it was fine; I was always her favorite, because my body looks exactly like her body! (Voice 3)

Basically I was close with my father's family—they're here in the United States. And my mother's family, they're in Japan, so I've only been to visit them twice—once when I was barely conscious of the fact that I was breathing, probably, and the other time when I was sixteen. They were great hosts, and my grandfather went out and every day he'd buy me a Coke, because that's an American drink. . . . The interesting thing is that my father never goes with my mother; she's been several times to visit. So there's a lot that is unspoken. . . . I don't know how my Japanese grandparents felt about my mother marrying my father, let alone my mother coming over to the United States to study. But with my father's side of the family we've always been close; I went and stayed with my grandparents every summer for a month. (Voice 39)

My mother's parents—I have an older sister who's all White and they were pretty up-tight about us. My earliest memories were [that] we were dirty—they would hug my sister, but they didn't want to touch us. And the relatives on the White side, we were pretty much banished from the family, so there wasn't much contact. The contact that we did have was very strained. It wasn't a welcome existence. My father's family was that kind of Black kinship network, so it was more warm and loving family gatherings—big cookouts and lots of fun as a child, but as I got older, it was harder, because I was more aware of the difference. As a child, I didn't know I was different. (Voice 40)

My mother's family—in Chicago, my great-great grandmother lived nearby and we used to go to visit her. I have really nice memories of going to see her . . . she always had lemonade in the summer and she was just very nice. . . . Her house was always like one of those White suburban homes with very clean furniture. . . . There were all these damn family reunions. I hated them so much, because we were the only Black people there. . . . It always made me feel really different. . . . My father's family I only visited once when I was a baby. My mom went down to Alabama after having me, and that's it.

I changed my name the summer right before my second year in college. . . . And I did it because I just didn't want my father's name any more, because I really had no connection to him or his family. It's not anybody's family name. I just chose [my last name]; I really liked it. I wouldn't have picked my mother's name, because I couldn't. First of all my mother changed her name from Smith, and then about seven years later she changed it, she picked her own name; she changed it to Aspen—no connection to anything except to something that was inside of her. Then my sister still has Smith. There's no way in hell that I would pick anything from my mother's family; I can't stand my mother's family. . . . I just wanted to have my own name, basically. People always try to make it something different; it was simple. (Voice 6)

Because of the divorce, my father's family pretty much wrote us off . . . with the exception of my grandfather who was just wonderful and my father's mother

who was also, but his sister and my cousins, there wasn't a lot . . . of contact. . . .
My mother's family, we were completely cut off from, because of the way they
looked not only at Black Americans but Americans, period. She left Japan to
marry my father who was in the service and they completely disowned her for a
long, long time. . . . As time passed and they lost her mother, . . . that opened
up the lines of communication again. . . . Even now, there're no calls to Japan, . . . although my mother is in close communication now again with her
sister and her father. (Voice 7)

Well, with my mother's family it was always pretty close. My dad's family initially—when my mom and dad got married, my father's Italian . . . and when
they said that they were going to get married, my grandfather would have
nothing to do with it. The whole family tried to talk him out of it. So in the beginning when I was really, really young, my dad kept bringing me over [to my
grandparents]. [When I was four or five,] my grandfather died and he was really probably the staunchest one. After that, almost every Sunday we would go
over to my grandmother's house. (Voice 12)

My mom's family was a White family . . . there were three sisters. We had family
gatherings every two years. . . . I remember thinking it curious that all these
people who barely ever interact with Black people in virtually anything and everything they do are having to interact so intimately with them. And finding
that odd, but not feeling that that affected the relationship. I know that initially when my parents got married, it did affect [it] tremendously. One of her
sisters wouldn't have my mom's name spoken in her presence for a year—the
other one didn't want it to happen but, once it happened, said, "That's okay, if
that's what you choose." (Voice 14)

My father is a White Jew from [the Middle West] and my mother's a Black
Baptist from [the rural South]; they tried very hard to allow me to know [their
families]. My father's father is a very, very good man and a very smart man but a
man who worked from day one to support himself and his family, who always
was a good provider, but because of that he took work to the nth degree. He'd
try to make an effort with us, but I think he never . . . felt comfortable around
us. Thus our relationship was very formal. . . . And when he passed away last
summer, the pain I felt was for my father. My father's younger brother made an
effort to be close to us. . . . A very good man, a very bright man, but not culturally sensitive as I am in my life right now, but I respect him for the effort he's always made. . . . My mother tried very hard to always have me know my
grandfather; my grandmother was deceased many, many years ago. I used to
spend part of the summer down there in the South. . . . I definitely have tighter
ties with my mother's side of the family. And I think that partly springs from
the fact that I'm Biracial; I'm perceived by society as Black. My mother's side
being Black, I have much more in common with them as far as race is con-

cerned and social life and cultural life. So that as I get older, I become more confirmed in dealing with that side of my heritage. (Voice 44)

Actually, there was some sort of controversy about me being adopted. . . . There were arguments from [my adopted father's] side of the family, because I was too light. My father's family said, "If you adopt her, she's going to hate us, because we are dark." And so they rejected me first; they didn't give me a chance. . . . With my mom's side of the family, it was great, everybody accepted me; my mother is dark and everyone in her family is dark too, but . . . they all embraced me, they were great. And I was old enough to know that I wasn't born into my family, but I never, ever felt bad about it; I was made to feel I was loved and chosen, so that was good. (Voice 32)

With my father's parents, they were pretty accepting of my mom when my parents got married, though now I can look back and hear stories and I know that—racism seems like a harsh word—but ignorance on their part. . . . And as for me, I was their first grandchild, so they loved and adored me, and I happened to be blond and very white. I don't think they would have been different if I had been a darker kid, but I wonder if they would have been so enchanted with me as they were. And then being enchanted with me, I loved them; I thought they were great.

And my mother's mother was in the United States for a while and we actually had a difficult relationship, because we are alike in a lot of ways. I was very talkative and very interested in things. My mother did not raise me in a religious background. My mother's mother was religious, so I was constantly challenging her views and thinking she was ignorant and told her so. I wasn't her favorite; she liked my sister, because my sister was more passive and more lovable and cuddly. (Voice 37)

COMMENT

Although respondents variously recall their relationships with parents and parents' relatives, some commonalities emerge in their remembrances. Children who grew up with both parents often consider that their relationship changed because of evolving racial identity issues or to such existential factors as illness, personality differences, and parental career demands. While children who grew up with parents perceive changes in their relationships with their parents over time, divorce often irrevocably disrupted relationships, not only between parents and children but between grandparents and grandchildren.

Although some respondents lived in the same houses with grandparents, others lived half a world away from them. Spatial propinquity, however, was less important to the quality of relationships with grandparents, uncles, and aunts than other considerations such as the parents' relationships with one another and personality compatibility. Families that initially opposed interracial marriages often mellowed over time to accept their Biracial grandchildren, nieces, and nephews.

Assessments of Biracial American Experiences

This chapter records selected responses to three related questions. The first set of questions asks, "How do you feel about your Biracial heritage today? What are its assets and liabilities? How did you feel as a young child and as an adolescent?" The second set of queries inquires, "Growing up, do you think that you encountered any special problems and special privileges because of your Biracial heritage? How about now?" The third question is the final one of a long interview: "Is there anything else that you want to tell me about your experience as a Biracial American?" The responses to these reflective assessment questions again display the experiential diversity of this group of young adult Biracial Americans as well as the power and poignancy of their voices. (See chapters 4 and 5 for a discussion of topics addressed in this chapter.)

ASSETS AND LIABILITIES OF BIRACIAL HERITAGE

I think growing up I was always very excited to be Biracial, because my parents were so excited during the sixties; they really felt that society was going to change. They were internationalists and my father was a Pan Africanist. They just really thought that the new society was going to be great and that they were like the best and the brightest of the Old World and the New World. And like my name, Hope—everything about me was in anticipation of this great excitement, of this blanketing of all the best and so I think I willingly stepped into that role—that this is great—I am a bridge—without thinking how incredibly exhausting that would be. It was nothing I ever regretted as a child and a teenager. Then for a long time—I think once I came to college I was resentful and I felt that all the models open were the tragic mulatta. . . . So now I don't feel one way about it or another, because it's just who I am.

I still feel the responsibility of being in a unique position to articulate that and get that story out and educate people about it, and educate the Black community about it as well. . . . My parents' party line was that all people are created equal only we just have to celebrate difference, instead of teaching me that racism does exist on institutional, personal, and cultural levels. I think that if I had been raised in a Black family, they would have given me those tools to be able to turn stuff away. And I feel that that is the problem with liberal Whites having Biracial kids or adopting Black kids and saying that, "Well, I can live with a baby of whatever color." . . . And my mother wasn't prepared to teach me what I needed to know. I don't think any White person can understand the profound level of [racism]. (Voice 9)

I don't have a Biracial heritage—I have a White heritage. I miss not having a father, but I don't miss not having a Black father. . . . I'm glad that I am brown, because I love my skin color. And I also think that it's been a really wonderful experience for me to be brown, because of the things that I'm interested in now in my life like issues of oppression. I'm not sure I would have those interests had I not had to struggle with them myself, so for that I'm really grateful and also I'm really grateful that I'm not White, because I don't want to have the guilt of all these years of oppression. . . . I have to deal with other issues, like issues about what is happening in the Black community. . . . But generally it was hard growing up. . . . And people who ask me now—people who say "Y'know, I'm thinking of dating so and so and he's Black and I'm White and what if there are kids?" And I say "It's hard to have children who are mixed." Because society sucks, but I don't think people should be naïve about that. I think it's very difficult. . . . As much as you try to share different cultures with your children, it's just really difficult to do that in the United States of America. . . . I think it's hard, because all the mass media messages say that it's better to be a White person. But I'm hoping that will change. (Voice 24)

I am really able to see that things are a lot more complicated than just Black and White, not only because there are other races and other issues like class, but because there's something really profound when someone has a close parent who is of another race, because it really makes you think about the whole idea of, "we can't love each other" or, "we can." It sounds really corny, but it does make you think differently about it, because you know that it's never that simple, there's always complicated things going on. So I think that that's the best asset that I have. . . . I think all identity is constructed; everyone thinks about what it is that they think being Black or being White or being whatever is and they act accordingly. You have a more heightened sense of that when you are Biracial, because you know that you can choose to be a variety of things. I guess the downside is that . . . I'm really sensitive to people questioning me or questioning my politics or questioning my identity. I feel very vulnerable to someone saying, "Oh, she's just White-identified." That's actually painful. It doesn't really come from White people and I probably wouldn't care if it did. But it's definitely more with Black people and it comes up in the context of who I've dated or who I do date, so it's a constant issue in that sense for me. . . . There's a constant shame in some ways that you're always facing. It's not like you can just, in this political climate, claim both parts of yourself and not choose; you always have to choose. So if you choose to say, "I'm Black," there's a constant shame, because you can't really be up-front about who you are without people saying, "Oh, she's just trying to let me know that she's half White." In college a lot of people dealt with that dynamic by being just as pro-Black as they could be and never, until graduation day, did you know that they had a White parent. . . . That part I think is the real downside of it.

I think growing up maybe I would have experienced it differently . . . if I'd had parents who were more interested in telling me how difficult it was going to be instead of just saying, "Oh, you're mixed; you're the best of both," emphasizing that special aspect which is really a negative thing later on. When you're five, it's great, because you're feeling insecure and you're feeling like, "Oh, I'm not fitting in in all these ways." But when you get older, if you internalize that, it fucks you up; it makes you feel a sense of "I am the best of both" without seeing how loaded that is in so many ways. So I think growing up I didn't have a sense of how complicated it was and the fact that there were all these people waiting for me to choose and waiting for me to fit myself in some category that they had assigned to me. (Voice 1)

Now I consider it a blessing. I believe that I have the best of both worlds. [When I was younger,] racial ideas were only going to cause me more conflict; it would have caused me more of a problem where I lived if I addressed them. . . . So repression was probably the rule by which I dealt with that. (Voice 35)

I wouldn't change anything at all. . . . I think it has more to do with my parents. . . . My parents are . . . hippyish—you know love, peace, and happiness. . . . You know, they have this vision that on earth there are really good people. But the point being that their friends are very multicultural—by seeing that and by having that context, I think that your perspective on what race is and the different kinds of stereotypes that you deal with—be it Asian or Latino—they're just not there for you, because you've had contact with these people. . . . So my parents are very tolerant and acceptant of all kinds of people, so we've had that in our lives. (Voice 2)

My personal view is that it is hard being a Biracial child, because I never felt like I fit into either. When I was around my White side, I felt I didn't fit in; and then when I was in the Dominican Republic around my cousins, again I felt very White and didn't fit in. I never feel like I belong to one particular group and I always wanted to; I always wished that I was 100% something. Now I concentrate less on it, because I'm just an individual, but I consider myself Hispanic. (Voice 3)

Today I've found that I do have a dual identity. I think that most Blacks also have a dual identity, but it's not to the same degree I have. . . . I can function in the White environment purely as myself, whereas other Blacks probably have to change or behave differently to function in the White environment and that I think is the key difference between me and a darker person. . . . The positive is that I slip into both environments easily and I feel accepted in both environments; the negative is that I often feel I'm not accepted in both environments. . . . I have been called too White or too light by some Black women to date and I know one White woman that I'm too light for.

When I was teaching woodworking over the summer, I was teaching troubled youth and some of them were Black. What happened was, I said something and one kid asked, "Are you Black?," because of the way I said it. And I said, "What do you think?" And then there was this debate among the Black kids whether or not I was Black. And when they discovered that I was, then they started playing with me. . . . I'm not as verbal in terms of the faddish dialect they're talking now and I'm not from the Philadelphia area, so they know that I'm not hip, but they also know that I'm kind. They don't know what to think of me. . . . I felt from that that there was a certain mixed—it's always a mixed thing—acceptance of me and also nonacceptance. I'm not really one of them, because I'm too light. And I'm too unhip or whatever; I'm not street enough. But there's a whole other thing—if you want to go into the difference between Blacks who are raised middle-class from the suburbs and Blacks who are urban-raised. So that's a major variable . . . that affected my relationship with the kids then.

And then I often run across situations where I feel good when somebody who doesn't know me—a Black male will walk down the street who doesn't know me and through a crowd of White folk will look at me and say, "What's up, Black?" You know, that sort of thing. And that confirms something in me and makes me feel good. It reminds me that I can be visibly Black. My brother I feel bad for, because he doesn't necessarily get that, but then again he hangs out in more Black circles than I do. So he is also more involved in the Black community than I am, so maybe that's helped him a bit.

[When I was a small child,] I never thought of myself as Biracial then. I wondered why I was light. . . . I think I always felt somewhat different everywhere. . . . I suppose being a child of the sixties that came right after the Civil Rights movement, I just saw the residual pride of that and grabbed on. . . . I think [it] has something to do with my generation. I think this new MTV generation probably has a different perspective on things and they will probably blur the lines even further. (Voice 45)

Now I think [my Biracial heritage] is great. I have a real interesting mix and . . . a lot of people comment on that and just the other day people were saying, "You could pretty much go almost anywhere in the world; a lot of places in the world people would have a question whether you might be from there. That's definitely an asset. Liabilities—just being in this society, having any African in you and having it be distinguishable can be a liability. . . . [As a child,] it was not the fact that I was Biracial, but the fact that I was light-colored and I got a lot of teasing, people used to call me "Banana Man," "piss colored," all kinds of stuff that had that kind of connotation, and a lot of it was from [Black] friends [beginning in the sixth grade]. . . . I didn't like it, but it wasn't a big deal. (Voice 4)

When I was younger, I felt all this pride; now being older, the sense of pride is replaced by a sense of how useful it has been. . . . I think of it as having prevented me from taking certain positions that a lot of people I know have taken. . . . I've never been able to take a side in racial matters. And I now see that as having been very useful in my learning to deal with the world, learning to deal with people in the world. (Voice 33)

As an adolescent I liked being able to have friends in the projects and not get beat up and to be able to know that my father was Black, I was proud of it, it was who I was. . . . What's interesting, if I'm around White people and they don't know I'm African American, they say things that they might not normally say. And, of course, that can be considered bad or ugly, but it's also very interesting. I may say something like, "Well, as an African American this is how I feel about it," and that lets them know that they're not talking to a White person and they can respond however they want to. Or I have a tendency to get a little pissed off; I have a certain way of seeing things and it's very black and white. When people start talking like that, it depends; I used to want to explain . . . but lately it's been like I don't want to be bitchy or mean but I don't want to be super nice and explain or help them understand; it's not my position to do that. (Voice 6)

Today I think [my Biracial heritage] is wonderful. There were moments when people isolate you and you are different and that's painful; you just hate being different; you just go through, "I just want to be normal," a little bit of that, and "I don't want people to look at me, because my hair is a certain way. I mean that's not who I am; my hair doesn't make me this person or my skin color doesn't make me." It was hard, because I wasn't fully accepted in the Black community and I definitely wasn't fully accepted in the White community. It was, "Where do you fit?" . . . There was a time where you hate being different; it's not that you hate your Black heritage or your Japanese; you really just want to be normal. . . . But that was real short-lived for me, because I just wanted to say, "Forget it." Junior high and then early years of high school—that was that period. But I quickly again decided, "Forget it, if they don't like me that's their tough luck; that's their shortcoming. I'm not going to let it bother me; I've got too many other places where I want to put my energy."

And today I want my kids not only to learn about their heritage but to learn about other cultures and nationalities, because I think it's really important that they don't limit themselves. . . . I am trying to help them to grow and to embrace all those different heritages. (Voice 7)

I think it's kind of interesting [being Biracial], because I sort of get to sneak up on people—Black people and White people. When they start talking about "those dirty Jews," I say "Well, excuse me." . . . I like it, because I'm different. I like that I see other people like me now more than ever before, and I really enjoy that. I know that [younger Biracial people] don't deal with it in the same way that I do; it was a different time when I grew up. . . . It's very reassuring. I think in a sense that I'm destined for a very lonely life in a lot of ways. I may never find a man that will understand me in the way that it's necessary to understand me. . . . It's not true for a lot of people who are younger and that's good.

The one thing that I try to really do on a daily basis . . . and I tried a lot harder when I was younger—is to break that stereotype that people who don't like Black people—and that's not only White people in America, there are a lot of people who don't like Black people in America—to break that stereotype of the ignorant welfare mother who would prefer to have children and do drugs than work, and I think that I'm a good counter example and I enjoy that a lot. I enjoy being able to hold conversations with people that don't expect me to be able to; I enjoy going to stores and talking to saleswomen who would really prefer to treat me or probably anybody else like they're less than, and I like that. (Voice 11)

My sense is that I didn't come away with a lot of self-confidence through all this or a secure sense of identity. I can recall watching a *Hill Street Blues* program—they had one of their high-level psychotherapy raps; all the head folks were talking about various problems they had. A Black guy came on and basically said that he wishes he was White; he wished he wasn't Black. And it angered me tremendously, because it's not him being Black that's the problem, it's other people being racist. . . . Because how I look at the world and how I relate to people, I feel that's a function of having been hurt a lot, and I have an attachment to the underdog that I believe came from my own appreciation and experiences of being oppressed. I don't necessarily like the word "oppressed," I don't feel that it's quite accurate, but certainly "victimized" by racism. And I wouldn't trade that; I like who I am that way, though I wish I had more self-confidence. (Voice 14)

I have no illusions about the access that my fair skin gives me, and my straight hair. I don't think in certain contexts that it makes too much difference, but I know that in many settings even before I open my mouth, I'm given the advantage. And yet my mind and my values are firmly in that multiracial landscape and I identify as a person of color and I feel profoundly out of the loop sometimes when a conversation is taking place, but I don't want to belong to that loop. Proud to be out of it.

My sense is that there aren't too many liabilities to being a well-educated, fair-skinned Latino these days. [My Biraciality] helps in my work enormously, to understand where different groups are coming from. What they value, not only what they need to hear but how they need to hear it; the politics of the context, not just the content. I think I've given some insight into that. And I draw on that daily.

I change my speech. I'm a lover of accents and an armchair student of culture and differences in how people use personal space and language and all those things, and sometimes it's quite conscious. I'm also conscious of not doing it in any way that someone can easily peg me as belittling them or patronizing them or humoring them. With changing the expressions that I use, I'll be briefer or more drawn out, I'll intonate a little differently, particularly when I'm with Bahamians at home, with African Americans in the South Bronx. It's something that I do consciously. (Voice 15)

There are times when I can use my latitude between communities to good account. I have a hyperrealized sense of the importance of race and looking at race and what race does. I have an appreciation for working toward something better. [Being Biracial] is a liability in the sense of the liabilities of being Black in this world, of being colored in this world, of being marked racially.

In some specific ways, I've never had . . . a preset package of rules either to rebel against or to adhere to. When I'm with my White family, the terms are okay; "Now I'm with my White family, what do I do with all this other stuff?" When I'm in my Black community, "What do I do with all this other stuff?" I think it's just about developing a strategy for living that's taken me many years and will continue to take me many years, and I don't think I'll ever be done. You know, almost anybody Black has to deal with some variation on this theme, so I think it's particularly painful for us. . . . Sometimes I feel I have to work harder to immerse myself in a Black environment than I do in a White one; I have to really seek out the Black environment. It's much harder than the White. Then coming from a White family, I don't think it's the same for people who had one Black family member. (Voice 16)

Today I feel proud of who I am; I feel good about who I am. . . . I just feel that all my life I've had different and diverse groups of friends and not had just one perspective on things. So I feel [that] it's an asset, because I'm open to these differences. And it's interesting—people who are mixed, we seem to bump into each other and cross paths. Although sometimes I feel that people who are just one race and one culture . . . maybe it would be easier. When I was younger, I used to wish more that I was just one, because then you could just say that's what you are. And I think I used to feel that if I just said that I was Black, then I was denying the Korean side. And then if I said I was Korean, I was denying the other side. . . . As I grew more aware of the fact that a lot of Black people have different heritages, I just felt, "Why not embrace everything?" (Voice 19)

The only asset [of a Biracial heritage] that I can think of is you don't really look like too many other people. . . . I think there are a lot of liabilities. You're never clearly identified with any ethnic group. You'll never be wholly part of any ethnic group. If I'm hanging out with Whites, then I'm Black; if I'm hanging out with Blacks, then I'm White. I've been told by Blacks on campus I'm too light skinned. There are plenty of liabilities. (Voice 48)

I feel good about [my Biracial heritage]; I wouldn't want it to be any other way. The only drawback is . . . sometimes I feel pressure not to identify Biracially. Not from Jim directly—it's not like we talk about it a whole lot, because we just consider ourselves Black. . . . Out of the blue sometimes he'll say, "You know, I don't consider you half White." And I'll say "Well, I certainly don't consider you half Japanese." It's just a Black thing with us. But I know for a fact that he identifies very strongly with being Black and if all of a sudden I said, "You know, I'm feeling really good about being Biracial and I want to fill out my forms like that when the census comes around. And when people say, 'Are you Black?' [to say] 'No, I'm Biracial.'" I don't particularly want to do that. But I feel . . . he probably would raise his eyebrows.

And I think what ties into it for me is the fact that I'm adopted. . . . One struggle for me about being adopted and being Biracial is that I feel that I have to deny it a lot of the time, because certainly my [adopted] mother and father are my parents and people meet them and I say, "These are my parents." In a way I feel that they certainly are my parents, but that doesn't tell the person who is meeting them truly where I came from; . . . before I knew I was Biracial, I didn't really feel that way. But now, especially with having a kid, . . . even if it's 90% of the representation of who I am and what I've become, it's not the whole story. . . . If my adopted mother happened to be White, then I suppose I would feel as though when I introduced them as my parents, the person I'm introducing them to would know them as these are the people who raised me and this is also the racial makeup of this person. And that's not the case. . . . I feel every time I introduce my parents, I'm hiding part of myself. . . . So it's something I have to deal with. (Voice 25)

It's always kind of fun to eventually be able to tell [people] that I'm Black, because that just wouldn't occur to them. . . . When I worked as an intern in an investment banking firm, there was a person there who finally came out and said, "What race did you say you were again?" I said, "Well, I didn't." . . . No, actually the question was, "What nationality did you say you were again?" I said, "Well, I'm American. If you're asking me what my ethnic origin is, that's a different question. Are you asking me that?" "Oh, yes, yes, right, right." "I'm Black." And his immediate response was, "No, you're not." And so the only other Black people there were a guy in the mailroom and the receptionists; there were no Black secretaries, there were no Black anything. I honestly think that reaction was that I went against everything that this person thought about what a young Black person was supposed to be, because I had a lot of respect in that place. Everyone respected my thinking, even though I was a very young person. [Not being pigeonholed is an asset, because] it forces people to approach me as an individual first until they can figure out who I am, eventually.

I think people should identify me as a Black person, because I certainly identify a White male as a White male, and there's nothing wrong with that. I think they should be sensitive to what I as a Black person might be concerned about, so you don't tell a Black joke when I'm there. . . . If someone does, I'll certainly say something about it.

And on the same token, one of the drawbacks of being of Biracial is that when I see a Black person, I'm not immediately identified as being Black. . . . When I see Black people, especially here in Sea Town, I want to run up to them and say, "Hey, guess what, I know you don't realize it but I'm Black, too, you can talk to me." . . . So that's a drawback; you feel that the people that you do identify with don't necessarily immediately identify with you and there's always this point of introduction that you have to go through. . . . This whole thing of belonging is something that haunts me and my siblings. (Voice 26)

I feel good about [my Biracial heritage]. I think my parents would have, even if they were both the same race, tried to expose me to a lot of things to keep me broadminded and put things in context. . . . I think the only questionable thing is—I think I was lucky—being young, I was very comfortable and probably did not have to worry or contemplate questions about race until I was more secure in myself, which I think was good, because thinking about those things when you're older is confusing. It's after college and my fiancé has . . . confused things a bit by raising questions, "Well, why are you Black? You're half White," which I find discomforting. I think if I say I'm neither White nor Black, then I'm mixed, but that doesn't feel good. I find being able to say one thing or the other is comforting. But [I'm] not saying that I'm not comfortable with being mixed; I am. If someone asks me what I am, usually I refer to being mixed, but on paper I say I'm Black. (Voice 27)

Right now I see [my Biracial heritage] as an asset, because I feel that I've been given the privilege to understand or to be someone special. . . . But the cultural part of being African American, I'm very proud of that, because . . . I feel that we have the freedom to express who we are a lot more now. And on the other side, being Asian, I feel that that's just as strong, even though I feel that's not quite [as] accepted on the Asian side as it is on the Black. Being Afro-Asian is a lot easier to accept if you're Black than it is if you're Asian. . . . The only problem is, you can't get full acceptance from either side, so that is a liability. I think it comes to a point where you have to be who you are and then find your place there.

As a young child, I remember feeling that it was really good that I have a Black father and a Korean mother; as a kid, I felt really special. As an adolescent, . . . the only problem was that I remember looking at other Black kids and my hair was not as coarse as theirs and my skin was light, so they would often look at me as not quite Black. Then living in the country, too, my mannerisms were different and my ideas were a little different. You could tell that I wasn't born and raised in a city or had those ideas, so that made it even more difficult. . . . When I went to visit my cousins [in Boston], the way they talked was different, because I grew up fishing and ice skating and doing everything that you do in the country; a lot of my cousins couldn't even swim. So they did not look at me, my brothers and sisters, as Blacks; they looked at us as mixed. It was cultural and racial. At that time I was trying to find out who I was or at least choose a side. But on either side I chose, I did not quite fit in. (Voice 8)

As an adult, I feel a lot of pride in coming from a Biracial background, because you really do learn about these two worlds. I think my parents have constantly given us throughout our lives—knowing both families and having exposure continuously throughout adolescence to both worlds—that there was always a comfort level in moving back and forth between those worlds. And they were very different settings. So now there's a lot of pride in that.

What's interesting now—I don't know whether it's because of society's awareness of Biracial people—African American people will sometimes ask me if I'm from a Biracial heritage because of the color of my skin. There's a lot more consciousness now. Or if I say I'm from a Biracial background, people will say, "Oh, yeah, I figured that." People are more astute in how they define this category that we call "African American."

As a young child and as an adolescent I definitely would not have said that I was proud; I was embarrassed. I would have said I didn't know what I was or how I defined myself or how other people defined themselves or how did I want them to define me; it was just a mess. (Voice 29)

[Being Biracial] does certainly make it hard to—you don't neatly fit in anywhere. That's the reality of being Biracial. I certainly have Biracial friends who don't see themselves as being Biracial; they see themselves as a member of one group . . . which means that they can be equally guilty . . . of making assertions that if they looked in the mirror, they can't really make. For me being Biracial means I can't make big sweeping statements, because life is very gray; life isn't just black or white, it's very gray. That's part of the asset [of being Biracial], that's what makes me who I am. I think of myself as Biracial person, I view myself as being in a Biracial marriage. I feel it is really important to me, in thinking about having kids, about how to give them the sense and understanding of their cultural and ethnic backgrounds, because they're going to have a really rich piece, which can help them. . . . So it's really something in my consciousness always.

I don't view living in [a White suburb] as a Biracial issue, but living there certainly created different kinds of issues for me as a Black person than it would have had I grown up in the city. In developing as a child, my initial entrée into groups of Black kids, I really was for all purposes, in term of mannerisms, in terms of tone, in terms of my language usage, in terms of the kind of music I listened to, I was White. It never barred me from ultimately developing relationships with people, but it certainly made it difficult in my own insecurities in my initial contacts with other Black kids who were from the city and their initial contacts with me. Always there had to be some point at which they basically made fun of me, because I didn't have any of what they viewed as Black characteristics, and we'd get over that and have a relationship. I don't think that was being Biracial so much as growing up in a White community.

My brother, sister, and I all grew up with our big old Afros . . . and I think the reality of that was that neither my mother or my father knew anything about hair. . . . All those pieces that are very much a part of the experience of being African American in this country, we just didn't have. That really at some level was a product of being Biracial also, with a mother who was White; if she had been Black and my father had been White, then who knows what my hair would have looked like as a kid. . . . Look, I'm terrified about doing anything else with my hair except letting it grow and going to get it cut all the time, but I have other friends who do all kinds of things with their hair; it looks great. I don't have a clue about how they do it, that piece of knowledge I just don't have. And that's part of being Biracial in the context of my family. I also do think the race of the parent does make a difference, but I also think it's about different kinds of hang-ups. I don't have a hang-up about "good hair" or "bad hair." That's not part of anything for me; now, that might be different if my mother was an Afro-American woman, because she might have grown up with some of those hang-ups and had that conversation. I mean the whole hair thing wasn't something I was tied into in terms of awareness of it until I was a teenager in terms of my camp contacts.

And also skin color—the idea that being a darker hue or a lighter hue made you more valuable or less valuable. That's another thing. I didn't have that baggage or those experiences, because again I really do think the dynamic of our parents didn't lend itself to that. To me that's a good thing.

But there are all kinds of little things like [that]. At some level, I guess it's the stereotypes that White people have placed on Blacks, that Blacks have incorporated into their own sense of themselves. At some level, it really didn't get passed down to us, and I think it's probably that for all of us the person who was most primary in our rearing wasn't part of it and it wasn't stuff that my mother adopted and decided that we needed to have. . . . So those are real assets in terms of not getting expectations or stereotypes of how we were supposed to be; we never really got them. And that's a really good thing. (Voice 41)

I feel [my Biracial heritage] has always been an asset, not a detriment. I've always had to prove myself, so if anything it's really helped me in school and it's helped me in my social life, and it's helped me in my career. I've always been very competitive. I don't know if that's due to the fact that I have to prove myself, but I always have to be the best at everything. Through running a contest—even in sales now, I have to be the best, and I always am. (Voice 49)

I don't think as a young child I realized that I was multiracial. I think that my parents did a whole lot with the idea that this is just normal; you are Indira and Indira doesn't have to be a category. . . . I don't think it's as problematic as people think it is. . . . People say having an interracial marriage is very difficult. I think [that] is a bunch of shit; that's usually rooted in a lot of insecurities and in a lot of archaic notions of what it means to love another person, to get married and start a family. . . . I think people who are very strongly against intermarriage have arguments that the children are going to be scarred for life—that's very primitive thinking.

I think there's something to the idea of not belonging. I know that I'm in a very privileged position. Not only from the fact that I had a pretty secure upbringing, but the fact that my mother's from Curaçao, which is a really small island but which is very, very racially mixed. Having a grandmother who's whiter than White and a grandfather who's not, and he isn't really Black but he's of African descent and also of Carib-Indian descent as well; carrying a lot more of those variables, I think it just matters less to me—the concept of purity and the essence of race; all those things affirmed me. So I think that was easier for me, but I can see in a larger world how other people might perceive that miscegenation will shut you out of a community and it's true. I have the luxury of saying, "Well, then you don't really need the community," or "You just belong as much as you want to and need to and move somewhere else or do your emotional needs somewhere else."

I think there are only a certain number of traumas you can handle in adolescence, and my big thing was my father's death and the subsequent death of a very good friend of mine in high school. I think that a lot of the emotional energy and developmental things that may have normally been channeled into worrying about my racial identity; instead, they were channeled into something totally different. I didn't do a lot of the wondering of where I fit in. . . . It's . . . more and more becoming a question now. (Voice 30)

As a young child, it was just horrible. In the sixties I did look White and other kids didn't want to play with me. And as I got older, other girls didn't like me and for a long time I did not have friends. And I think it was largely because of how I looked, [and] probably also because my mom is a teacher, she made me speak standard English all the time, so much so that it may have been more [significant] than the way I looked. But I was always being criticized. "You are so proper; you're so proper, why do you speak like that?" Well, I knew that the retribution of going home and speaking slang or being sloppy in my language would be much harsher than gaining their friendship, so I just had to make a choice to save my life. So when I was younger, [my Biracial heritage] was really a liability; it did not help me at all.

When I got to the dating stage, boys liked me but I didn't like boys for a long time. . . . I wanted girl friends, because I didn't have any brothers or sisters and I was kind of lonely. . . . When I talk to people today, . . . I am constantly surprised by . . . the view that a lot of Blacks buy into that lighter skin and straight hair are attractive; [my mother] never, ever let me think that I was anything special. . . . So I guess that as an adult, it's been helpful, because some people view the way I look as better. (Voice 32)

I've always liked [being Biracial], because it sets me apart. . . . Everything that I am is because I am both; I am who I am. . . . The fact that I look White, I don't think that it could ever mean something bad for me. . . . I've always been very proud of it. . . . Recently . . . it's not something I bring up to people, it's something that I think about; if I've gone out on a couple of dates with someone and it comes up . . . then I wonder if this person will have a problem with it. It's not something that I think about much. I've never found anyone who had a problem with it, so I've always been happy that I'm both. (Voice 42)

During adolescence it was hard, because you're trying to fit in. . . . You're just one away from being what's the right sort of thing. . . . But being Biracial . . . was hard. I actually like going to funerals and weddings—any family gatherings, because then I can see all my cousins and really feel part of the community. And my friends were of various mixes but mostly White and there wasn't that grounding; on one level I felt really close to these people, at the same time it just wasn't, I can't describe it.

Now, it's weird, because . . . a fair number of my friends are of mixed backgrounds. One roommate is Brazilian and Italian and my other roommate's mother is White and her father is Black, and my roommate Paul is Dominican but always pretty much seen as African American. So there was a sort of bonding on those things and being able to laugh at a lot of the stereotypes. And I think actually growing and being comfortable and coming to terms with, "[Y]ou can't chop me up into those little things—I am what I am." I'm thinking of that song, "I am what I am." But, you know, trying to encompass that, trying to include it all, because all of us have tales of our immigrant mothers not understanding and saying this . . . and hearing someone else having these tales and actually doing this oral history. . . . My mother hasn't been so open yet to let me actually tape her, but actually being proud of her and thinking of what she has done—leaving a family and an entire culture and coming here, and yet she and my father aside from the racial mix seem fairly mainstream, which is actually kind of funny. . . . And you know, I'm interested in getting to know what my mother was like, because it's understanding her and understanding me. Also understanding my father. (Voice 39)

As a young child, I don't think I thought [about being Biracial]; as an adolescent, I think I felt the same way that I do now, except that my coping mechanisms were different. I think as an adolescent, I knew that it gave me this perspective—I felt really special. I felt that I could see the world in ways that other people couldn't. And I knew that that was different and I knew that that was valuable. I knew that I would really need that throughout my life. But I also knew—and sometimes it made me feel really lonely. I felt like I didn't belong when I saw nationalism. . . . I became very involved with Black American culture, because it was something I could grab on to. . . . I went through a period of, say, fifth, sixth grade where the majority of my friends were African Americans; I read everything I could about Martin Luther King, Malcolm X, and then I picked up Black slang at the time. And I felt very comfortable with my Black friends and did not hang around with the little Hispanic kids. I did not hang around with the White kids. . . . It lasted throughout my life where I have actually had a real strong inclination towards Black culture and probably know a whole lot about it. And in college I did the same thing; in college I was very active in the Latino community but I was always clear that it was very important to bridge with the African American community, that also comes from being in New York where the Latinos and the Blacks are always trying to work together although always fighting over [political turf]. . . . And being able to move in different worlds, because I can move . . . I became, my mother said, her little Black child all of a sudden, because of that happening so early on and knowing so much about African American culture. I feel very comfortable around Black folks and I feel very comfortable around Latino folks; I feel least comfortable about a totally White environment, though my high school experience did prepare me for it. (Voice 37)

I feel that I have insights into a lot of things. . . . I think of Biracial people as a metaphor for the potential of these two sides—whatever the two sides may be—having been forced to really integrate themselves and to learn how to get along or to see the other side of the fence. And so I see myself as straddling the fence and having a lot of negotiating skills because of that. One thing that makes me sad, and I don't think it has to be this way at all—just something that happened to me that I would try never to do if I ever had Biracial or multiracial kids—is that my parents never acknowledged it.

Not only that, but they got divorced and now they are remarried into their respective races; . . . we [my sister and I] found out about both marriages after they were married. I just think that is terrible. . . . Now my sister and I are the only . . . visible evidence that that interracial marriage ever existed and we are sort of the proof. (Voice 36)

SPECIAL PRIVILEGES AND PROBLEMS OF BIRACIAL HERITAGE

Privileges—maybe yes, because the only thing that I can remember is, when I look back now, the teachers that I had and somehow I remember feeling like an exception but I didn't really know an exception to what. . . . Problems—I think about race a lot. I think about what it means to me a lot. I think about why I spent a lot of years being really angry that things are the way they are, because you know, we grew up in this world where people are good . . . and we had really positive experiences and then when you wake up and [you discover] . . . there are bad people in this world and there are horrible things that happen—I mean I was really angry for a long time. And then I was angry about the fact that a lot of bad things happen to people, because they are Jewish or because they are Black and it's like it's just hard to identify with something like that; you think, how can you deal with something like this? And so I spent a lot of time being really angry about it and so now I think about it a lot in terms of what that means to me and my future. (Voice 2)

Certain things in life, it's hard to know whether to attribute them to the Biracial element in my parents' marriage or just to their personalities, but sometimes I do feel there were a lot of problems, because my dad was not . . . an American person at all. . . . He just seemed so weird to us. . . . I think that a lot of the things that I took as him being mean or being a bad dad were really cultural differences. He really thought that if he was in China, people would be saying what a great father he was. . . . Looking back, it was a privilege to me even though I grew up in such a sheltered town to even just walk into those Chinese people's houses and to have a taste of another world inside my own town.

Now [a friend] and I have talked about this problem—of wanting to reach out to other women of color or Asian women, for me, and finding that when I am with Asian women sometimes, I feel that I'm not really Asian, but then, of course, when I'm with White people, I don't ever feel White. . . . I'm so much wanting to have the approval of these Asian women that I'm not able to just relax and be myself. (Voice 36)

I had a recent experience. . . . I needed some work and I didn't know what it was about but there was a foundry job in the paper and I went down there . . . [to] a working-class White neighborhood. And this old Polish man about seventy-five comes to the door. And he's a rascal of some sort. He's got his gutter language and his rough talk and he's of that blue-collar gutsy kind of generation. Well, he was starting to like me for the job and we're talking about it and I told him about some of the things I did. I think he was happy to find somebody who could speak and didn't care about getting up early, 'cause I was telling him "Oh, yeah, I can get here at six, if you really want me to." So I was excited about the whole thing. Then he started talking. . . . Then he said, something about that "nigger lady." I said "What?" He said, "That nigger lady on TV, what's her name? The one with the talk show." And I looked at him for a while, I didn't say anything. He said "Anyway, I was listening to that." Then he started to say some gutter thing. And I said, "Did you know I'm Black?" And he said, "Naw, I didn't know you were Black; I didn't know you were." He said, "Don't mind me." Then he started to try to make up for it, "Don't mind me. That's the way we used to talk. I don't care what you all say. I don't have"—then he was going to say, "I don't have any prejudice whatsoever. I call myself 'Polack,'" and then he was talking about the Jew up the street and [then] he calls everybody this and that. And then I said, "Don't be calling him that and don't be calling me that." He said, "I don't think of you as Black." And then I said, "I don't think I want to work here," and left. . . . But that's the kind of experience someone with my color, my complexion can get. Whereas if I were darker, he wouldn't let me in the door; he would probably say that the job's been taken.
   People let me in a little more easily; they do not see me as Black. . . . I, therefore, probably didn't get shut out of things like I think other people are. For the most part, I didn't feel necessarily any overt racism; it would have to be blatant. I felt much less racism than, for example, my cousins. One of the negative things is that when you do get the racism . . . you get to hear it. I remember when I was eighteen going to bars . . . and that's when you meet the worst people. Hanging out with my buddies, whose other buddies would join us and these people would start talking trash and then I would have to remind them that I am Black and they would say, "Oh, I didn't mean anything by that.". . . . I guess that's primarily the racism that I encountered—somebody saying something stupid, not knowing what I am.
   One of the other things that the older generation of Blacks—which is a sad thing—and I felt that this has affected my life. I was doted on because of being light. . . . We were pretty kids when I look back at the pictures . . . , but even still, part of what made us pretty to Blacks was our lightness and that was something that Mom didn't like to see happen, . . . but we ended up being the edu-

cated part of the family—my cousins are well-educated too, but still not as educated as my brother and me and we tend to be the ones who have achieved the most, but Mom was the more educated one but then again she married White. There was a lot of that sort of thing that was in our consciousness . . . but when we are out in the Black community going out to dinner, to a function—I try to maintain a low profile, because I'm educated enough to be fairly articulate. . . . So my concern is that I'm not perceived as elitist. So I have to downplay myself sometimes and my brother downplays himself really well. He will hang out with buddies and no one will know that he's an Ivy League grad with a Ph.D. . . . I'm a little more arrogant; I try, I try, but I can't do that as well. That's one of the things we're conscious about. . . . He's good at . . . humbling himself so that he doesn't allow his 'brother,' his Black friend, to be uncomfortable with his achievements. That's an important thing for us. (Voice 45)

Special problems—I think a lot has to do with self-image. All through high school people probably thought I was confident, and I was confident on a certain level, but then there's that other side of it—just physical appearances and coping with that as an adolescent. And just sort of trying to reconcile affirmative action. . . . When you think about it, to me a lot of where I am happens to be because of my class. Affirmative action is necessary but . . . you can't get up to that certain point where affirmative action does you good unless you've come through the system. I went to an all-girls Catholic school that was a college prep school and I did well on the SATs, because I had that training. . . . I remember a friend of mine telling me—she's half Indian and half West Indian and I remember she was standing in line freshman year and some guy who's tall and White turns around and comments to his friend as he kinds of scans the room and says, "I guess they were really serious about affirmative action, because you know they're a lot of different people here." And she took it as a slight, because that was the fact that got these people in, not that they were intelligent or have different perspectives that were their assets and different talents. . . . And so that's always a running thing [to deal with]. (Voice 39)

Well, perhaps I got some privileges when I think back. I had to work when I was younger. We didn't have a lot of money. I worked as an usherette and I would take people to their seats at the theater and the ballpark. I always got really good jobs—I worked at the ballet and I got to see all the plays. I never thought that maybe I was getting plum jobs . . . it never occurred to me that I was the only Black person around. . . . One day a Black woman that worked at the same office said, "Would you take a job for me? I can't go." Her job that night was to stand up in the middle of a ring and hold up cards at a wrestling match. It was horrible. I said, "What a horrible job." And she said, "Oh, they always give me horrible jobs." And I had no idea; I said "Wow, I get these great jobs!" As I look back, I think I was able to get better positions. (Voice 32)

Being perceived as Black, there was a tendency to exoticize me; "she's so cute," "she's such an articulate little Black child," or things like that, so I got special attention. . . . Being the only Black gave me a little special category, not so easily pigeonholed. (Voice 9)

[Growing up,] I felt I had to prove myself a little bit more with the Black community. That's where I feel the most accepted and at home, but I also think it's harder to feel okay there, but once I'm there I'm happier. And with the White community it wasn't a problem. . . . Now I think [being Biracial] is more of a privilege than it's a problem. I think I don't scare people as much, because I don't look like what they think Black would be. And that's something that probably gets me into easier conversations with people. Actually from there I see problems sometimes, because . . . ignorant things are said, because they don't necessarily think of me as having feelings about being Black as strongly as I do. But otherwise it's probably easier to not fit into people's stereotype of an African American person. (Voice 13)

Maybe the "privileges" are an access to resources that many Black people don't have and a sense of entitlement to White culture. . . . I would always hear—this is a litany that most of my mixed friends have heard—"Oh, you're not really Black." "Oh, you're special; you're special." We've heard that so much: "You're special." What are you really saying when you say I'm special? Are you saying, "You're closer to White so you're better"? (Voice 16)

The [privileges] could have come out of being fair skinned. I wasn't aware of these things originally, but I've had people make me aware of them. People treat me a little nicer than they do a friend of mine who's brown skinned, because I happen to be a little lighter. You know, how they treat you paying a bill or buying something. I guess sometimes it does help, but I like to think it's my personality. (Voice 5)

I was unique and different and so I think that caused a lot of attention, just because I was one of the few Black students; I was different in the sense that I was lighter skinned than most of the other students. The Black students would point out to me that I would get treated a little bit differently. . . . I would get compared to the other Black students; "Oh, your hair is softer." Black students would come up and say, "You've got good hair;" I'd say, "Every hair that covers your head is good hair." Then realizing that the softness was perceived as something they wanted. I wanted what they had, I wanted the kinky hair like everybody else. They wanted what I had.

  I can also remember starting high school. . . . The counselor wanted to put me in the slow lane, because I was Black, with all the other Black students. . . . So my parents addressed that. . . . They just wanted to assign us to the easy lane to get us through, and the counselor even thought he was doing us a favor; but really what he was doing was cheating us—cheating us in life; lowering our expectations for ourselves. And that could have an everlasting effect. (Voice 23)

[Growing up,] I think that I was the chosen one; in my classes I was definitely the token Black, but I like to think it was because I was bright. However, that may not be the case. And in [graduate] school now, I know that I am definitely one of the chosen people, because of my skin color. And it's very difficult, because it puts that much more pressure on me to be successful and to be really, really bright. But I look at the University and there're 2,000 tenured professors and twenty of them are Black, and I say, "I don't really care; I'll take their money; this seems a little bit ridiculous." So I think that you get chosen for things and you become a token person and that is hard, because then you don't know for sure if it's your ability or if you're just being favored because of what you look like. But then you look at the group starting and you weigh the costs and benefits of buying into the system, because of course I'm buying into the system if I'm accepting race-based scholarships. But I'm hoping that the end of my work will be more important than how I got there. It's hard; there's a moral question there. One of the people who mentored me in terms of helping me get into [graduate] school . . . said, "Jennifer, there are so many people who are bright who don't get places, because they're so worried about how they get there, just get there and then do big things." Well, I thought that was good advice. (Voice 24)

[One problem is hearing] certain comments about Blacks by non-Black people. In a way I like it, because I get to hear a side of people that they [wouldn't show when] they're on their best behavior. . . . It's an opportunity to try to educate them. . . . So I guess in a way it's a privilege but in a way it's a burden. I don't see any outright privileges other than I do think that White people seem to be more comfortable with you if they perceive you as being more like them and not only education-wise or job-wise or goal-wise but if you can add on top of that, appearance—the texture of your hair, the length of your hair, the color of your skin, or if you have light eyes. . . . I've had people say "What are you mixed with? You're so light." And I'm light, that's true, but I'm not that light. I've seen a lot of Black people an awful lot lighter than I am. . . . There are a lot of people lighter than I am whose parents are both Black, so it's a lack of experience or worldliness [that makes people say those things]. (Voice 25)

Being Biracial always makes it easier for us to move into many circles that other people might not. . . . I think that what being Biracial does is it allows you to live in both worlds. There are two Americas, one Black and one White. You can move pretty freely between both while not really fully connecting in either and it gives you more insight. . . . And unfortunately [you're on the margins] that's where you live. I can see where it would screw a lot of people up as well, so I think you have to make a decision. You've got to be one or the other; I don't think you can be both. . . . I don't think we can make up an entirely different race like in South Africa and just call us the coloreds or something. . . . I don't think that's right. (Voice 26)

Just back to being in [graduate] school, I don't think that a lot of the White people here realize the way that society and school and everything just cradles them. I realize that people take things for granted and I'm not saying that I wish to be White, because I certainly don't, but some of the privileges like just looking on the TV and seeing yourself, seeing yourself in this wonderful life, having this feel-good White curriculum that validates who you are and tells you that you come from somewhere great. Then when you talk about Blacks all you talk about are ghettoes and racism and problems and alcoholism, and teen pregnancy—all these negative things in school when they have a Black course or a racism course.

When I talk with White people, I have to talk in their culture and their language. I can't speak to them in patois or in Black American English. I can't talk to them about certain things that are not part of their cultural experience. . . . All of my Black things have to be put aside and all of those have to be done only in the company of my Black friends. (Voice 28)

All my friends were White when I was a kid and I'm sure that if I was darker, their parents would not have quite let me in their houses. Because my features were a little bit different and my skin was and my hair wasn't as coarse [I think] that it was easier for them to accept me in the house. Even though I found out that there was a limit to that, because as a kid I used to go over to my friends' houses all the time and that was fine, their parents had no problem with me coming over. But I remember one time that I was going to go out on a date; I must have been around twelve or so. I was going out with my friend's sister and his mother objected to it. That was one of those quick shocks.

Now I am very proud of who I am and what I have done. . . . Even to this day, my wife and I go places and I can still feel racial tension in stores; sometimes we'll go in and they'll ask to help people and then they won't ask me. . . . The way I look at it now is it's not my personal problem, it's what other people have. (Voice 8)

[Special privileges] because of my African American part, yes. The first time I sensed it was when I was accepted to the University of New Hampshire and my [White] boyfriend wasn't. It was very interesting to me, because he had better SATs, though I was a stronger student than he. There was no reason why he shouldn't have been accepted. (Voice 29)

I've never had a problem with the fact that I was half Korean and half American. In fact, I always enjoyed that aspect of it; I liked the fact that people couldn't figure out where I was from. The only thing I had a problem with was someone being prejudiced and calling me names. And I got to be pretty tough, because of it. I think, if anything, it's enhanced my life and made me a much stronger person. (Voice 49)

"Whenever I've had to identify myself, I identify myself as White. I could never say that I was Black, because I'm not. It's part of what I am but it's not [predominant]. . . . You can look at me and I'm the reason that sort of racism is just so incredibly stupid is that if my appearance is White, it is who I am. If I'm treated differently, if people assume different things about me because they thought I was White; the people who sit there and have known me and thought they were my friends but don't know who I am and sit there and say things; when they find out who I am, it's, "Oh, but you're different." That to me has always been a [problem]. (Voice 42)

Well, it's commonly held by Black people that the fairer you are, the less African your features, the greater your privileges and access to White society. Though because I only live in one body I have no way of knowing what would have happened had I been darker, thicker lips, broader nose. . . . It's also hard to separate physical characteristics from something like my speaking voice, which is a clear Queen's/King's English, and I don't speak the vernacular unless it's appropriate, depending on the context. So it's hard to know if it had anything to do with my parents' racial backgrounds; it had to do with the fact that I went to private schools. . . . Growing up, there was a sense occasionally expressed by friends that I wasn't entirely Black . . . it didn't affect much and it didn't have as far as I know any crushing psychological impact. . . . Right now I'm not sure. I can only guess what my existence might be like if I look differently, if my background were different. I know what is said about skin by Blacks, but it's hard to know what it has really done for me. (Voice 33)

I can recall some feeling. . . . My Black relatives and friends reinforced that [with,] "Oh, he's got good hair." . . . They had anointed me as being prettier, because I had more European or half-way European, half-way African features. I think I did have problems, especially growing up in [a suburban] setting . . . where I simply just was so ambiguous to people and I just had a feeling of not fitting in. I still struggle occasionally with being in settings where I think people might be looking at me or wondering about what my background is. (Voice 38)

I think that the problem came with the non-White side. I think that institutionalized racism affected me, because a lot of people could look at me and say, "You don't look like a minority"; things are set up in such a way that if you are non-White, you'll get caught in the system. So to me that was a problem. . . . Had I not been mixed, I would not have experienced institutionalized racism. And then I can look at it from the other perspective of the privileges—since

I'm not minority looking, I have White-skin privilege. . . . I knew that early on.
. . . I chose not to take advantage of it, and I think early on because of my loyalty to my mom, that I definitely did not want to be treated special, because I
had White-skin privilege. And I am the lightest in my family. My sister is not
dark, but she is more identifiably different. (Voice 37)

I'm not sure if it was because of my Biracial heritage, but I did encounter a lot
of special privileges. . . . Growing up, I was always put in that leadership role.
And a lot of responsibilities were also given to me earlier. . . . [Today] sometimes I do run into other Blacks who have a problem or don't understand . . .
why I have White friends. . . . But I feel confident about who I am. If you have a
problem with that, that's fine; you go ahead and do your thing, I'm going to
do mine. If you can't deal with it, just don't try to push your attitude on me.
(Voice 34)

There was always the sense that—I think I'm the same way, I respond to Biracial children much differently than I do to non-Biracial children; I'm really into
them; I love them all; I think they're the cutest little children, and I feel this in-
stant empathy for their road. So I give them a lot more attention and love, even
though I don't know many. But when I see them, I find myself doing that. And
I think to some degree that people did that with me and again it's hard to tell
how much of it's because I'm Biracial and how much of it's because I'm Sarah.
But they're not separable, so who knows! . . . For example, my teachers when I
was in elementary school responded to me in that way; people were very enthu-
siastic and caring and great. As I got older, . . . I could feel a twinge of that em-
pathetic response, that sadness, that hurting and loving, but, "God, what a
hard road she's going to have."

Privileges—as I got older, I went through a long period of having long dred
locks; I fit into the exoticized Biracial woman à la "Flashdance." I got a lot of
strokes or appreciation of response, because of that kind of exotic beauty that I
was participating in to some degree. At this point it's hard to tell, I have so
many signifiers. . . . I'm doing work right now within feminism and trying to . . .
[broaden] our notions of what is empowering for women, also trying to revi-
sion the movement to include women of color. . . . I think that to some extent
White women feel comfortable with me because I'm not Black, so that can as-
suage some guilt or some feeling that they should be relating to a Black woman
yet I'm White, so there's this comfort level. . . . And I don't think they feel that
they'll be as judged or there's room for them . . . and I think that's a real privilege. . . . I don't know if privilege is the right word, but it's certainly a result of
being Biracial.

Problems, well, I still feel the same twangs of, "Maybe I'm inferior to everyone," when I go to my White family's dinners. . . . And then I think it's so hard
for Black people to imagine being Black and then having this White father. So

there's a way in which it doesn't compute and you still feel different from Black people. (Voice 43)

REFLECTIONS ON BIRACIAL AMERICAN EXPERIENCE

I would never in a million years change the way I grew up. . . . It has made me who I am. I like that. I don't like it when I let things get to me—that you need to be a skinny little White girl or, "Why can't you look like that?" . . . that happens a lot. I think that's one of the worst things—how you get looked at by the men on the street or what the TV tells you or your work place tells you. . . . I don't like how that makes you forget the very simple truth, which for me is, "I am totally kicking and I love the way I am and I love the way I grew up and I wouldn't change it for anything." (Voice 6)

My story is the absence of any Black people until all of a sudden at nineteen being in a place where you look Black, so you're supposed to know what that means. . . . I think it's interesting to see how much garbage professed by the media goes into thinking that there is one Black experience and that it's a very rough street sort. . . . What does integration look like? Because for me it still seems to be a seesaw back and forth—now in this way I'm White, now in this way I'm Black, and is that African American or is it Nigerian or is it Ibo or whatever? And is it really White, because it's a marginalized White—it's a poor working class immigrant White. . . . Now the swings aren't as dramatic as they were when I was younger, but is there ever an actual interweaving or does it mean that you'll be doing constant swinging back and forth? . . . I even knew friends who knew that I was struggling with being Biracial who didn't even tell me they were Biracial. I found out later they weren't just Black but they were Biracial. I don't know if they don't have that category in their minds, if, to them, they are Black. [Perhaps] it was too dangerous at one time for them to say that they were Biracial, so they just decided that they were Black and had forgotten everything else—I don't know. (Voice 9)

I really feel empowered by my identity and I think if we could all understand the world in terms of people being multiracial, we could break down a lot of the barriers of difference that divide and really sabotage our ability to live in peaceful coexistence. So I get a lot of power thinking of myself as a person of [my] world. And a person who embodies the blurring of divisive lines that I think it's going to take to change the world. (Voice 43)

One of the things is that I don't know too many Biracial people. And the main thing is that I'm operating in a primarily White culture. Often when I do feel that I've been immersed very far in White society and I feel the need to get back in touch, then I'll call somebody in Detroit. . . . I think the major thing I surmised while talking to you is that when you're light, you have to make an effort and when you're light and removed from the environment, you have to seek actively belonging. I don't know too many light Blacks who will actively seek belonging in the White environment, 'cause it's easy. . . . Now dressing, I've discovered, affects the way people treat me. I know that's class. (Voice 45)

I've been referred to as "mulatto," or "Biracial," or "interracial." And I don't think of myself that way. And [that] comes from an understanding that it is purely a social definition that is based upon some erroneous thinking in terms of the larger public thinking about groups of people. But given that we can't come to some logical way of thinking about human variation, I have just grown to take comfort in the fact of my identity. And I suppose this is due to the fact that my father wasn't around. I have never really thought of myself as being from different backgrounds. Because background implies a culture. So while I have genes from many different parts of the world, my background and what I know from my family and what I've been taught, what has been passed on to me, and where my head and my heart are, is with an African American identity. (Voice 38)

Sometimes I see myself in a unique position to bring people together. Oftentimes when I've encountered non-Blacks, they don't know that I am Black and I've actually known people for months and interacted and been friendly and then it's discovered, "Oh, you're a Black person," and I think to myself, "This is great, because this person can see that I'm not so different, and maybe I've built a bridge here." So I like when that happens, for some reason.

When you think about interracial people and Black people, I think I find that more troubling, because within our race we have people who are so mired in old ideas, and you find that people either fawn all over you and think that you're really beautiful or they hate you. (Voice 32)

One of the things I've thought is that it's always like being on the outside looking in, especially in terms of the majority. Middle-class Black Americans are raised with that. I feel devoid of cultural history and it's not altogether bad; I feel that I have to make my own way, because there was no strong effort to go one way or the other. It took me a lot more effort in the past to be comfortable; it takes a lot less effort now. There was a time [in college] that I cursed my parents for ever having me, because I just went through so much trying to figure out who I was and it was almost as if I didn't have a choice. Really what it was was coming to accept myself as I was and for who I was, but I cursed them; I hated them for putting me through this. "Why did you do this to me? Why did you make me different?" (Voice 11)

Probably because of where I've lived I haven't experienced [prejudice] as much as other people may have, which is good, because it made it easier. But I have experienced enough things that I know what it must be like to have it be more. I've always thought—and I probably got this from my mother's family. They grew up in a section of Applebee that was predominantly Italian. And at that time Italians weren't all that highly thought of in Applebee; yet my mother's family was accepted there and taught to speak Italian. My mother's family always had the attitude that it was who you were and what you did and those were the important things and not what race you were, and I think they projected that so much that I think it helped my family get so well accepted. My uncles were very talented musically and everyone in the world knows the Samuels and the Sitwells of Applebee. . . . There are always going to be problems out there, but if you dwell on them, it's going to make them worse. And for me I think that we have to get beyond where somebody comes into a room and says, "There's a Black guy, there's a White guy." . . . We've had people come into Applebee and say, "Applebee is a bunch of bigots," and I think, "is this the same place I'm living?" And people can dwell on all that stuff; that holds them back. (Voice 12)

Since [my early twenties], I've had to very consciously grow closer to a "Black community" and close to my Black identity, but then also to be able to accept the specific kind of Black person that I am. I have White family, I have White friends, and I have this Whiteness. And the reason that I hesitate to say "integration" or "peace" is that it is not a peaceful process, because I have this war zone inside of me and I always will, and it's never peaceful and there's always friction and some sort of confrontation that will go on in my life, no matter what. If I'm with my White friends, I feel comfortable with them in a certain way but not in other ways. And when I'm with my Black friends, I'm comfortable with them but not in other ways. And I have to put up with shit from both sides. Some White people will say ignorant things or they won't know things, or I have to listen to different sets of problematic kinds of things. So I would very much hesitate to say "peace," but maybe "negotiation." (Voice 16)

[When I was born,] I feel everybody was really into the idea of having these beautiful Biracial kids (and it's hard to find a not so good-looking Biracial kid—the blend is just magical), but I don't know if people realized being challenged and not really belonging to anybody, not being embraced or claimed by anybody, but in fact having to embrace and claim yourself and sort of project that onto whoever it is Black or White, whatever you decide to do. (Voice 28)

I think Biracial Americans seek out other Biracial Americans. I've found that with almost everyone I've encountered, except maybe there are some that deny and want to be accepted. There are some people, you'll ask them are they mixed and they'll say no; they just want to be one or the other. They'll say, "No, I'm not mixed; I'm Black" or "I'm not mixed; I'm something else." And I think they go through that where they can't deal with it, so they just want to be accepted as one thing or the other. (Voice 47)

I'd say [being Biracial] opens doors and I truly believe that's a big part of it. Why? Because this is a racial country. They label everyone differently. . . . I think it has a lot to do with culture as well as race. . . . There're times when I'm going out and I'm working with customers and they're predominantly a bunch of White guys and we might just discuss anything in general and they might look at me and make a comment. "Yeah, you're different from other Black guys." Then I say, "In what sense?" And they say, "Oh, you're not really Black." You know, in other words, you're an "oreo." And I take offense to that. So I think there are different experiences that I have had as a multiracial person. (Voice 21)

As a Biracial American, it's rough out there. It's hard to live on the line; it's hard to be African American on the one hand and still try to understand and really appreciate the other half of who I am. . . . And it would be nice if I could actually be both things. But I can't. At least, I don't feel I can. (Voice 5)

I never felt that I had the choice of being identified as Biracial. I felt that I couldn't identify as White. I pass—people have thought of me as White a few times. When I was in high school, if I wore a hat and didn't have facial hair, a couple of times it happened, and that's only people whose perception of Black is very, very dark skin and different from the people who I spent time with. I think when I was growing up people weren't identified Biracially and it's unfortunate. And [the increase in multiracial groups] is positive, but . . . there have been many conservatives who say, "Well, it's just more Blackanization, political correctness." But I think it's nice to represent what they're about. And I've never been in a situation where I could choose [to be White] and frankly I wouldn't want to. I'm very happy with who I am. (Voice 44)

I'm sure that any kids who are mixed have a difficult time at adolescence, when a person picks his friends, and he picks what he believes in, and he picks his life, because it's all part of his identity. But as a Biracial kid, I think we have more of a stumbling block, because we're not accepted very easily by our friends, we're not accepted by our own races. . . . My son is mixed and I can tell him he's "Black," then my wife says he's "Spanish," and then my mother—he tells his Asian friends that he's "Korean." He values it all. He's not dark, he's light skinned, his hair is pretty fair, so I'm sure that at some point in life, he's going to have to pick a certain root. But I've learned, because I have tried to pick roots and each root that I've picked was not satisfying for me. One time I wanted to see if I was Black all the way and it wasn't there for me; then I went to the Asian side and it wasn't there for me; so then I went in between; when I met my wife it was a Spanish way, but that wasn't me either. So at this point in life I decided well, I'm just Afro-Asian, that's who I am. (Voice 8)

I think for me personally, one of the things I struggle with is kids. I mean, you're Biracial and you're in a Biracial marriage—if my kids are light-skinned enough that people will identify them as White, would somehow they feel less connected to me, because we weren't the same race? It's almost a fear that they would feel less connected to me. I've thought about that. And I think back to my own experience and I don't have the capacity to have any sense that I would feel any more or less connected to my mother if she were Black or not; she's mom and that's kind of it.

My racial identity is an important part of who I am. I'm more conscious and aware of that since college and law work than I ever was growing up. I didn't have that kind of political consciousness about my race; I just didn't. . . . So . . . when you think about kids and you think about your life and how you're going to lead you life, it plays a real role in it, in a way that people who aren't Biracial never at some level have to think about. I can't imagine that two White parents ever think about what their race means and the race of their kids means for their kids and how they forge relationships.

I think it's interesting, this cohort of Biracial kids who are five or so years younger than I am who check off "Black and White" or "Asian and White" or "Hispanic and White" on their forms. It's a whole different way of constructing yourself than anything I would ever have thought of. I sometimes wonder about, why did you allow yourself to be so boxed. They wrote on your birth certificate. . . . Somebody defined you and at some level you continued down that path of being defined within that group. Why did you do it? Why don't you make a choice not to adhere to that? But that doesn't seem to have mattered to me. My conception of myself is, "I'm a Black person"; that's just who I am.

I'll be really interested to hear the different perspectives of people from different Biracial configurations. Most Black people can look at me and know that I'm Biracial; most White people haven't a clue; some Latinos, they're a lot more sensitive about Biracial—because their skin color runs the gamut. So because White people and the people who have most of the power that I come into contact with don't know that I'm Biracial, most of the experiences I have are a result of being a person of color, not as a result of being Biracial; experiences that I have within the Black community are a combination of the two at different times. That's a different experience from someone who's clearly in one camp. So I'm interested to see if that's true for other [Biracial configurations].

For me, being Biracial is much more about how I think about myself and how I think about how I want my children's life to be and how I want the world to be, because for the most part the way I'm treated in the society, I'm treated because I'm a person of color and I'm a woman and not because I'm Biracial. (Voice 41)

It's incredible. And I'd stress again that I think it's particularly in the latter half of this century and only for a certain class bracket. . . . You know, my mom used to say, "We are the color of the future." And that's such a beautiful thought, in a way. It's also a very depressing thought, because it could mean the death of cultures. . . . When I was younger, I really did think we were a future group. But as I grew older and began to read history books, I realized how long we've been around. And so I mean politically that . . . makes me Black. Mentally, it's been tough, because I've always wanted to be accepted by the entire population of Black people and have sometimes found that difficult, and that's very painful. . . . I have problems with the Man. Sometimes I feel closer to Jimmie Baldwin than any other writer that I've read; I haven't read anyone recent who's talking about the same stuff, which I think describes what the issue of raciality really is. And that it's not necessarily your pigmentation, or your parents; it's your placement. (Voice 31)

Biracial incorporates so many different things. You can be a Biracial Asian. . . . I think maybe Biraciality involving an African and something else is more significant than any other Biracial [combination]. . . . Life experience is no monolithic thing. It's experienced in different ways depending on your situation. . . . Black experience in America is different from Chinese American or Native American. (Voice 20)

When I talk to other people that have been through this experience, the thing that stands out for me . . . about the way I grew up was that my parents weren't— a lot of people who are Biracial, their parents were these radical people in the sixties and got together through that impulse—and my parents weren't like that. They were very middle class, fairly conservative. . . . I think that's why race wasn't talked about, why a lot of that stuff went unexplored for me, whereas with other people that I know it's more the case that one of their parents—usually the person who is Black—was very conscious about telling them all these things and the other parent either would listen or just ignore it. In my family it was different, because my father didn't really talk about things much; it was more that he led by example. . . . He was an attorney who would perform legal services for Black people who couldn't afford to pay him . . . or he belonged to Black organizations and he didn't really talk about it. . . . My mom was high-school educated and lived in Black neighborhoods a large part of her life and had a lot of Black friends, so she was really used to talking about race and so she would talk to me about things a lot. . . . It was weird, because she was the one who was much more willing to talk about race than my father was. (Voice 1)

COMMENT

The responses to these evaluative and reflective questions illuminate some of the major life themes of these young adult Biracial Americans.

While most respondents state that as adults they find their Biracial heritage to be an asset in which they take pride, many allude to feeling that it was problematic during their childhood and adolescence. The issue of not belonging to a single racial and ethnic group is perceived as both an asset and a liability. It is an asset in enabling one to take a more complicated view of social realities, to function in multiple sociocultural worlds, to act as cultural "straddlers," or to play simultaneously the roles of insider and outsider. At the same time, however, a Biracial person does not fit into a sociocultural category or may feel pressure to identify with one racial heritage and not another. At least one respondent does not find "Biracial" to be a meaningful designation, given the overt and covert complexities of racial constructs. Another anticipates that the next generation of Biracial Americans will further blend racial categories.

In responding to the issue of special privileges and problems associated with a Biracial heritage, many participants focused on colorism, exoticism, code switching, and racial rejection. Several mentioned both the privileges and problems associated with being light skinned, including being both doted upon by European American teachers and relatives of color yet hearing racist comments intended for European American ears, receiving better jobs than darker skinned friends or than European American friends yet finding it harder to have African American than European American friends. Others mentioned the negative aspects of being considered "exotic" as an adolescent and as a young child, while others noted their facility in switching cultural codes and moving easily in different sociocultural worlds. Nevertheless, a number remarked on the racial suspicion if not hostility and rejection that they received from both European Americans and people of color.

Given the opportunity to provide some additional information at the end of a long interview on racial identity and life experiences, various themes emerged, including differentiations between race and culture, reflections on the nature of biraciality, and identity choices for oneself and ones children. A number of respondents affirmed the experiential primacy of culture over race, such as the man who asserted that whatever his genetic makeup, "Where my head and my heart are is with an African American identity" or the young woman of Asian/European American parentage who stated, "Just because this person looks like me doesn't mean that we have anything in common if we can't even communicate with each other." Others affirmed the empowerment that their Biracial identity creates for them, while another reflected on her experience of the dialectical interweaving and polarizing of racial identity. Yet others reflected on the choice of a Biracial identity rather than a monoracial identity of color, considering that the former may be a more prevalent option among the next generation of Biracial Americans. These comments provide significant insight into aspects of the Biracial American experience for those of the post–Civil Rights generation.

Epilogue

This chapter reviews the major findings of this study of young adult Biracial Americans and presents some concluding observations on Biraciality and the deconstruction of race in America.

A TRANSITIONAL COHORT OF BIRACIAL AMERICANS

The young adult Biracial Americans whose life experiences with race and racial identity issues have been probed in part I of this book and whose voices have been recorded in part II represent a transitional cohort of Biracial Americans. Since they were born in the 1960s and grew up in the 1970s and 1980s, they had their formative racial identity experiences before Biraciality was as widely acknowledged in American society as it is today at the opening of the twenty-first century. They are thus betwixt and between the hidden generations of the past and the visible blended generations of the future.

The young adult Biracial Americans with whom I talked are diverse in the sources of their Biraciality. Their parents include European Americans and Europeans, African Americans and Africans, Asian Americans and Asians, Latinos and Caribbeans. Moreover, they have had varied formative racial identity experiences as a consequence of their diverse family structures and socioeconomic statuses, the racial and socioeconomic mix of their growing-up communities and schools, their peer relationships, and their own idiosyncratic natures. In addition, they have made different life choices with respect to career and life contexts. Most have experienced turning points in the development of their Biracial identity. The timing of such turning points varies from person to person; not even siblings reared in the same household experience them at similar times in their lives. Today most of these young adults identify themselves monoracially as people of color, some identify themselves Biracially, and a few identify themselves as European Americans. Nevertheless, despite the diversity of their racial heritages and sociocultural experiences, they share the experience of being Biracial people in a society dominated by White culture.

As Biracial people within a White hegemonic society, these young adults share certain important existential commonalities, including ambiguous racial identities, color conundrums, and racial rejection. Their ambiguous racial identities are both a source of comfort and discomfort; they confront and variously resolve sociocultural conundrums associated with skin tone; they often find that they are visible as Biracial people to people of color but invisible to European Americans; they experience racial rejection both from European Americans and from members of communities of color; they often have struggled alone with racial identity issues; they have changed their racial self-descriptors over time; and they acknowledge the lifelong impact of negative racial childhood encounters. Yet they are racially cosmopolitan in their choices of friends and spouses.

While sharing such existential commonalities, these Biracial young adults' personal views and experiences are diverse. Part II records the range of responses to some interview questions, revealing not only differences in life situations and personal experiences but variations in social orientation and societal understanding. Certain project participants articulate a complex comprehension of Biraciality within the context of American society, others a less sophisticated and more personalized view of their experiences as Biracial Americans. Such differences are attributable both to personal development and personality and to socioeconomic and educational opportunities.

BIRACIALITY AND THE DECONSTRUCTION OF RACE

When as Americans we think about race, we tend to think in terms of invariant and discrete categories. At any given time our national census categories summarize our collective racial map, which changes as society changes. But census categories, like all categories, are mental constructs that human beings imbue with meaning. Our current census categories indicate that as a society we are beginning to differentiate between race and ethnicity. Biraciality, however, is a construct that does not exist among the current census categories. Until the 2000 census, the census has demanded that a person identify as a member of a single discrete racial category.[1]

When we Americans think about race and culture in our society, we tend to think in terms of Black and White, of African American and European American. Although this polarity disregards the complexity of race in America, it reveals the framework within which much of our racial experience is interpreted. As a society, we value Whiteness over Blackness. All Americans participate at some level in this evaluation. Many of the Asian/African Americans with whom I spoke talked of their own experience in terms of White and Black, although that did not describe their natal heritages. White and Black are the poles between which all other racial modalities range.

When thinking about race and culture in American society, we tend to assume that people who look alike necessarily share a common culture. But as one Asian/European American woman living in San Francisco said,

A lot of the Asian people in the Bay Area, actually their first language is not English and so it's been hard, because I moved out here with the great feeling about being around more Asian people. It's also been good . . . to remind me that race is a rather arbitrary thing and it turns out that . . . language is a really big difference. Just because this person looks like me doesn't mean that we have anything in common if we can't communicate with each other. (Voice 36)

Culture and class, then, intervene to create heterogeneous social realities within racial categories.

When thinking about race and culture in American society, we tend to think monoracially. We assume that a person who appears to be European American is European American or one who is brown-skinned with very curly dark hair is African American. We often do not entertain the notion that they may identify themselves in some other way, perhaps as European American and Asian American or European American and African American. Biracial people often take pleasure in others' inability to pigeonhole them; at other times, they may feel that they belong everywhere and nowhere in American society.

When thinking about race and culture in American society, we tend to forget that almost all Americans are indeed multicultural if not multiracial and that there is greater biological diversity within "races" than between the different strands of humanity. As one young woman who during her lifetime has identified herself successively as "Mixed," "Black and White," "Puerto Rican," "Spanish," "Black and White," "African American and Jewish," "European American and African American," and now "European American, African American, and Native American" said, "If we could all understand the world in terms of people being multiracial, we could break down a lot of the barriers of difference that divide and really sabotage our ability to live in peaceful coexistence" (Voice 43).

In the future, we can hope that all Biracial Americans will be able to claim as their own Maria Root's "Bill of Rights for Racially Mixed People." These rights as Root presents them are:

I have the right

>   not to justify my existence in this world
>
>   not to keep the races separate within me
>
>   not to be responsible for people's discomfort with my physical
>   ambiguity
>
>   not to justify my ethnic legitimacy

I have the right

>   to identify myself differently than strangers expect me to identify
>
>   to identify myself differently than how my parents identify me
>
>   to identify myself differently than my brothers and sisters
>
>   to identify myself differently in different situations

I have the right

>   to create a vocabulary to communicate about being multiracial
>
>   to change my identity over my lifetime—and more than once
>
>   to have loyalties and identify with more than one group of people
>
>   to freely choose whom I befriend and love[2]

Were this bill of rights adopted by Americans of all races, not just mixed-race Americans, many of the problematic issues that Biracial young adults today confront and have encountered during their lifetimes would disappear. The quest for a confident sense of self as a Biracial American would not be so arduous. One would readily claim one's place in a multiracial and multiethnic America.

NOTES

1. With the 2000 census, Americans will be able to choose multiple racial identities. While this opportunity represents a new societal recognition of biraciality, its results have yet to be assessed.

2. Maria P. P. Root, "A Bill of Rights for Racially Mixed People," in Maria P. P. Root, ed., *The Multiracial Experience* (1996): 7.

Bibliography

"Are the Children of Mixed Marriages Black or White?" *Jet*, 21 May 1990, 52–54.

"Black America and Tiger's Dilemma." *Ebony* (July 1997): 28–30, 32, 34, 138.

"Break Bounds: Interracial Couples Smash Stereotypes." *Times* (Essex County Newspapers), 9 July 1991, B1–2.

"Changing Colors." *Mother Jones*, (September/October 1997): 38–54.

"'Colorblind' Goal Blurs Race Issue, Clinton Told." *Boston Globe*, 8 July 1998, A13.

"Feeling Our Way: Talking About Race and Identity in America." *Radcliffe Quarterly* 83, no. 3 (Fall/Winter 1997).

"Interracial Baby Boom." *Futurist* 27, no. 3 (1993): 54–55.

"√Other: Portraits of Multicultural Families: Resource Guide." Cambridge: Multicultural Arts Center, 1994.

"Rally Held for Multiracial Category on 2000 Census." *Boston Sunday Globe*, 21 July 1996, A21.

"The New Face of America: How Immigrants Are Shaping the World's First Multicultural Society." *Time* (Special issue), Fall 1993.

"The New World: A Special Issue on Multiculturalism." *Boston Globe Magazine*, 13 October 1991.

"US Marriages Between Races Now 1 Out of 50." *Boston Globe*, 12 February 1993.

Adiele, Faith. "Learning to Eat" / "The Multicultural Self" /"Remembering Anticipating Africa." In *Miscegenation Blues: Voices of Mixed Race*

Women, edited by Carol Camper, 362–376. Toronto: Sister Vision, 1994.

———. "Standing Alone with Myself." In *Life Notes: Personal Writings by Contemporary Black Women,* edited by Patricia Scott-Bell, 364–388. New York: W. W. Norton & Co., 1995.

———. "Finding Faith." *Revival* 2 (1995): 13–16.

Alphonse, Lylah M. "Race Needs 'Other' Option." *Boston Globe,* 5 October 1996, C1.

American Anthropological Association. "AAA Statement on 'Race.'" *Anthropology Newsletter* (September 1998): 3.

Arboleda, Teja. *In the Shadow of Race: Growing Up as a Multiethnic, Multicultural and "Multiracial" American.* Mahwah, NJ: Lawrence Erlbaum Associates Publishers, 1998.

Association of Multiethnic Americans. "Testimony, Before the Subcommittee on Census, Statistics and Postal Personnel of the U.S. House of Representatives" (Washington, D.C., 30 June 1993).

Atkins, Elizabeth. "When Life Isn't Simply Black or White." *New York Times,* 5 June 1991, C1, C7.

Bannister, Erin. "The Meaning of Mulatto." *Radcliffe Quarterly* 83, no. 3 (Fall/Winter 1997): 33.

Barnicle, Mike. "No Colors, Just Three People." *Boston Sunday Globe,* 23 September 1990, 28.

Barringer, Felicity. "Mixed-Race Generation Emerges But Is Not Sure Where It Fits." *New York Times,* 24 September 1989.

Bass, Alison. "Activist with a Beat [Malia Lazu]." *Boston Globe,* 2 November 1999, D1, D6.

Begley, Sharon. "Three Is Not Enough: Surprising New Lessons from the Controversial Science of Race." *Newsweek,* 13 February 1995, 67–69.

Bennett, Philip, and Victoria Benning. "Racial Lines Recast by New Generation: Greater Interaction has Failed to Span Divide: Young Americans, Black and White." *Boston Sunday Globe,* 13 September 1992, 1, 30, 31.

———. "Questions of Race Confound Anew: Young Americans, Black and White." *The Boston Globe,* 14 September 1992, 1, 6–7.

———. "Reconciling Principles, Racial Identity: Challenge Is Seen in Greater Diversity: Young Americans Black and White." *The Boston Globe,* 16 September 1992, 1, 8.

Benson, Susan. *Ambiguous Ethnicity: Interracial Families in London.* Cambridge: Cambridge University Press, 1981.

Berry, Karin D. "Adoption, Race & Red Tape." *Emerge,* April 1995, 40–44.

Biddle, Frederic M. "PBS Examines Blacks' Color Consciousness." *Boston Globe,* 15 February 1994, 26.

———. "When Color Lines are Drawn within a Family." [June Cross] *Boston Globe*, 26 November 1996, E1, E8.

Billingsley, Andrew. *Climbing Jacob's Ladder: The Enduring Legacy of African-American Families.* New York: Simon & Schuster, 1992.

Bleecker, Marcus. "My Father's Black Pride." *New York Times Magazine*, 15 October 1995, 34, 36.

Bradshaw, Carla K. "Beauty and the Beast: on Racial Ambiguity." In Root (1992), 77–88.

Bransetter, Ziva. "Black and White." *Philadelphia Daily News*, 15 February 1994, 1-6, 7, 10.

Brazelton, Dr. T. Berry. "Easing Biracial Concerns." *Houston Chronicle*, 17 April 1994, 7G.

Brennan, Patricia. "'Captive Heart': Writing a Happier Ending to a Tragic Story." *Washington Post*, 14 April 1996, 7, 43 [tv review].

Campbell, Bebe Moore. "Hers: Brothers and Sisters." *New York Times Magazine*, 23 August 1992.

Camper, Carol, ed. *Miscegenation Blues: Voices of Mixed Race Women.* Toronto: Sister Vision, 1994.

Cardwell, Diane. "Crossing the Great Divide: Writers Straddling Ethnic Identities Ask Who They Are and Where They Fit In." *New York Times Magazine*, 22 June 1998, 20.

Caryn, James. "Kinship and Skin, and Which Is Stronger." Review of "Secret Daughter," by June Cross. *New York Times* 26 November 1996. (Response to program.)

Chambers, Veronica. "Fredi Washington the Tragic Mulatto." *New York Times Magazine*, 1 January 1995, 27.

Chandler, David L. "In Shift, Many Anthropologists See Race as Social Construct." *Boston Sunday Globe*, 11 May 1997, A30.

Clark, G A. "Fixin' Racism." *Anthropology Newsletter* (March 1998): 7.

Cohn, D'Vera. "Census Race ID Policy Is Set." *Boston Globe*, 11 March 2000, A3.

Comas-Diaz, Lillian. "LatiNegra: Mental Health Issues of African Latinas," In Maria P. P. Root (1996), 167–190.

Cose, Ellis. "One Drop of Bloody History: Americans Have Always Defined Themselves on the Basis of Race." *Newsweek*, 13 February 1995, 70, 72.

Costa, Peter. "A Conversation with Elizabeth Bartholet: Fighting for the Right to Adopt Children Without Regard to Race." *Harvard Gazette*, 31 January 1991, 5–6.

Coughlin, Ellen K. "Sociologists Examine the Complexities of Racial and Ethnic Identity in America." *Chronicle of Higher Education*, 24 March 1993, A7, A8.

Crouch, Stanley. "Race Is Over: Black, White, Red, Yellow—Same Difference." *New York Times Magazine*, 29 September 1996, 170–171.

Cross, June. "Secret Daughter." WGBH *Frontline* Program (1996).

————. "Secret Daughter." *The Radcliffe Quarterly* 62, 4 (Winter 1997): 26–28.

————. "Making *Secret Daughter.*" *Abafazi: The Simmons College Journal of Women of African Descent* 8, no. 2 (Spring/Summer 1998): 55–61.

Daniel, G. Reginald. "Passers and Pluralists: Subverting the Racial Divide." In Root (1992), 91–107.

————. "Beyond Black and White: the New Multiracial Consciousness," In Root (1992), 333–341.

————. "Black and White Identity in the New Millennium: Unsevering the Ties That Bind," In Root (1996), 121–139.

Davis, F. James. *Who Is Black?: One Nation's Definition.* University Park: Pennsylvania State University Press, 1991.

Faulkner, Jan, and George Kitahara Kich. "Assessment and Engagement Stages in Therapy with the Interracial Family." In *Cultural Perspectives in Family Therapy,* edited by James C. Hansen, 78–90. Rockville: Aspen System Corp, 1983.

Ferber, Abby L. "Exploring the Social Construction of Race." In Zack (1995), 155–167.

Fernandez, Carlos A. "Government Classification of Multiracial/Multiethnic People." In Root (1996), 15–36.

Fish, Jefferson M. "Mixed Blood." *Psychology Today* 28, no. 6 (Nov./Dec. 1995): 55–61, 76, 80.

Fong, Rowena, Paul R. Spickard, and Patricia L. Ewalt. "Editorial: A Multiracial Reality: Issues for Social Work." *Social Work* 40, no. 6 (November 1995): 725–728.

Forbes, Jack D. "The Evolution of the Term Mulatto: A Chapter in the Black-Native American Relations." *Journal of Ethnic Studies* 10, no. 2 (1982): 45–66.

————. "The Manipulation of Race, Caste, and Identity: Classifying AfroAmericans, Native Americans and Red-Black People." *Journal of Ethnic Studies* 17, no. 4 (1989): 3–28.

Frankenberg, Ruth. *White Women, Race Matters: The Social Construction of Whiteness.* Minneapolis: University of Minnesota Press, 1993.

Freeman, Marc. "Student lst to Be Listed Multiracial." *Palm Beach Post,* 26 August 1995, 1A, 8A.

Funderburg, Lise. "A Woman of (Some) Color." *Mirabella* (May 1994): 76–77.

————. *Black, White, Other: Biracial Americans Talk About Race and Identity.* New York: William Morrow, 1994.

Gill, George W. "The Beauty of Race and Races." *Anthropology Newsletter* 39, no. 3 (March 1998): 1, 4, 5.

Gillespie, Peggy. "√Other." *Boston Globe Magazine,* 24 April 1994, 12–15, 26, 27, 32–36.

Givhan, Robin. "Interracial Couples Still Finding Opposition in American Life." *Boston Sunday Globe,* 11 November 1990, B31, B32.

Gordon, Albert I. *Intermarriage: Interfaith, Interracial, Interethnic.* Boston: Beacon Press, 1964.

Gordon, Lewis R. *Her Majesty's Other Children.* Lanham, MD: Rowman and Littlefield Publishers, 1997.

Gose, Ben. "Public Debate Over a Private Choice: Interracial Dating at College Angers Many Black Female Students." *Chronicle of Higher Education,* 15 May 1996, A45, A47.

Gregory, Deborah. "What Color Is Love?" *For Women First,* 26 April 1993, 50–53.

Haizlip, Shirlee Taylor. *The Sweeter the Juice.* New York: Simon and Schuster, 1994.

Hall, Wade. *Passing for Black: The Life and Careers of Mae Street Kidd.* Lexington: University Press of Kentucky, 1997.

Hamilton, H. J. Belton. *Christmas and Thirty-three Years Inside an Interracial Family.* N.p.:H. J. Belton Hamilton, 1990.

Hartigan, John, Jr. "Establishing the Fact of Whiteness." *American Anthropologist* 99, 3 (1997): 495–505.

Haygood, Wil. "Race in American life: Ideals Giving Way to Reality." *Boston Sunday Globe,* 14 September 1997, A1, A30–31.

Henry, William A. III. "Beyond the Melting Pot." *Time,* 9 April 1990, 28–31.

Hoffman, Paul. "The Science of Race." *Discover* (November 1994): 4.

Horowitz, Helen Lefkowitz, and Kathy Peiss, eds. *Love Across the Color Line: the Letters of Alice Hanley to Channing Lewis.* Amherst: University of Massachusetts Press, 1996.

Huber, Patrick. *Two Races Beyond the Altar.* Boston: Branden Press, 1976.

Jacobs, James H. "Identity Development in Biracial Children." In Root (1992), 190–206.

Jacobson, Matthew Frye. *Whiteness of a Different Color.* Cambridge: Harvard University Press, 1998.

Jefferson, Margo. "On Defining Race, When Only Thinking Makes It So." *New York Times,* 22 March 1999, B2.

John-Hall, Annette. "A Mixed Heritage and a Keen Eye." *Philadelphia Inquirer,* March 1994, B1, B2.

Johnson, James H. Jr., and Walter C. Farrell, Jr. "Race Still Matters." *The Chronicle of Higher Education,* 7 July 1995, A48.

Johnson, Kevin R. *How Did You Get to Be Mexican?: A White/Brown Man's Search for Identity.* Philadelphia: Temple University Press, 1999.

Jones, Charisse. "Debate on Race and Adoptions Is Being Reborn." *New York Times,* 24 October 1993, 1, 35.

Jones, Lisa. *Bulletproof Diva: Tales of Race, Sex, and Hair.* New York: Doubleday, 1994.

Jones, Lisa, and Hettie Jones. "Mama's White." *Essence* 25, no. 1 (May 1994): 78–80, 150–152, 154, 158.

Jones, Rhett S. "Race is Always *A Family Thing." Massachusetts Faculty Development Consortium Exchange* 7, 1 (Fall 1996): 2–3. (Response to film.)

Jones, Vanessa E. "A Rich Sense of Self: Many in New Generation of Biracial People Reject Narrow Categorizations." *Boston Globe*, 29 February 2000, A1, A7.

Kich, George Kitahara. "The Developmental Process of Asserting a Biracial, Bicultural Identity." In Root (1992), 304–317.

Kilson, Marion. "Themes from the Biracial American Experience." In *Claiming Place: Biracial American Portraits*, edited by Max Belcher, Marion Kilson, and Theresa Monaco, 1–3. Boston: N.p., 1995–1996.

———. "Themes from the Biracial American Experience." In *1997 Handbook on Race Relations and the Common Pursuit*, edited by R. Judith Coquillette, 9–13. Cambridge: Harvard College, November 1996.

———. "Hindsight: Biraciality and the Deconstruction of Race." *Sextant* VIII, no. 1 (1998): 24–30.

King, Rebecca Chiyoko, and Kimberly McClain DaCosta. "Changing Face, Changing Race: The Remaking of Race in the Japanese American and African American Communities." In Root (1996), 227–244.

Koch, John. "A Daughter's Story in Black and White: Documenting a Life of Crossing and Recrossing Racial Boundaries." [June Cross] *Boston Sunday Globe*, 24 November 1996, N1, N7.

Korgen, Kathleen Odell. *From Black to Biracial: Transforming Racial Identity Among Americans*. Westport, CT: Praeger Publishers, 1998.

Krebs, Nina Boyd. "Edgewalkers: Heirs to Many Cultures, Multihued Youth are Creating an Identity of Their Own." *Utne Reader* (September/October 1999): 75–76.

Kruger, Leondra R. "Multiracial Students: Searching for a Voice." *Harvard Crimson* 202, no. 79 (May 19, 1995): 1, 3. (Reply by Martin Kilson, 202, no. 91, June 5, 1995, 2.)

Ladd, Michael C. "Scarsdale on My Mind." 1987.

Laird, Cheryl. "The Ten Years in Black and White." *Houston Chronicle*, 17 April 1994, 1G, 8G.

Lawrence, Michael Jude. "Mixed Blood and Politics: The Role of the Mulatto in Black American Politics." Cambridge: Harvard College, 1988.

Lawson, Carol. "At Home with Marian Wright Edelman: A Sense of Place Called Home." *New York Times*, 8 October 1992, C1, C6.

Lazarre, Jane. *Beyond the Whiteness of Whiteness: Memoir of a White Mother of Black Sons*. Durham: Duke University Press, 1996.

Lee, Felicia R., "Youths Dare to Explore the Mine Field of Race," *New York Times*, 31 July 1993.

Leslie, Connie. "The Loving Generation: Biracial Children Seek Their Own Place." *Newsweek*, 13 February 1995, 72.

Leslie, Kent Anderson. *Woman of Color, Daughter of Privilege: Amanda America Dickson, 1849–1893.* Athens: University of Georgia Press, 1995.

Levine, Judith. "The Heart of Whiteness: Dismantling the Master's House." *Voice Literary Supplement* (September 1994) 11–16.

Lind, Michael. "Melting Pot Still Bubbles: Despite What *Multiculturalists* Say, USA Isn't Becoming 'Balkanized.'" *USA Today*, 8 August 1995, 11A.

———. "The Beige and the Black." *New York Times Magazine*, 16 August 1998, 38–39.

Macpherson, David A., and James B. Stewart. "Racial Differences in Married Female Labor Force Participation Behavior: an Analysis Using Interracial Marriage." *Review of Black Political Economy* 21, no. 1 (1992): 59–68.

Mahdesian, Linda. "'It's Not Easy Being Green.'" *U.S. News and World Report* 103, 23 November 1987, 8.

Mar, M. Elaine. "Secondary Colors: The Multiracial Option." *Harvard Magazine*, May/June 1997, 19–20.

Marks, Johnathan. "Black, White, Other." *Natural History* 103, no. 12 (December, 1994): 32–35.

Marriott, Michel. "Multiracial Americans Ready to Claim Their Own Identity." *New York Times*, 26 July 1996, 1, 7.

Martin, Antoinette. "It's Not Black & White." *Detroit Free Press Magazine*, 9 October 1994, 6–8, 10–12, 16–17.

Martin, Phillip W. D. "Devoutly Dividing Us: Opponents of Interracial Marriage Say God Is on Their Side." *Boston Sunday Globe*, 7 November 1999, D1, D2.

Mathabane, Mark and Gail Mathabane. *Love in Black and White*. New York: Harper Perennial, 1993.

Mathews, Linda. "More Than Identity Rides on a New Racial Category." *New York Times*, 6 July 1996, 1, 7.

McCabe, Bruce. "Interracial Intimacy: A Curious Candidate." *Boston Globe*, 12 October 1994, 71.

McBride, James. *The Color of Water: A Black Man's Tribute to His White Mother*. New York: Riverhead Books, 1996.

McDaniel, Antonio. "The Dynamic Racial Composition of the United States." *Daedalus* (Winter 1995): 179–198.

Minerbrook, Scott. "The Pain of a Divided Family." *U.S. News and World Report*, 109 (December 24, 1990): 44.

————. *Divided to the Vein: A Journey into Race and Family.* New York: Harcourt Brace, 1996.

Minton, Lynn. "Is It Okay to Date Someone of Another Race?" *Parade Magazine,* 15 December 1991, 16.

Morgan, Dodge D. "Further Studies in Black and White." *Maine Times,* 17 April 1992, 14.

Morganthau, Tom. "What Color Is Black?" *Newsweek,* 13 Feburary 1995, 62–65.

Morton, Patricia. "From Invisible Man to 'New People': the Recent Discovery of American Mulattoes." *Phylon* 46, no. 2 (1985): 106–122.

Moses, Yolanda. "An Idea Whose Time Has Come Again: Anthropology Reclaims 'Race.'" *Anthropology Newsletter* 38, no. 7 (October 1997) 1, 4.

Motoyoshi, Michelle M. "The Experience of Mixed-Race People: Some Thoughts and Theories." *Journal of Ethnic Studies* 18, no. 2 (1990): 77–94.

Mukhopadhyay, Carol G., and Yolanda T. Moses. "Reestablishing 'Race' in Anthropological Discourse." *American Anthropologist* 99, no. 3 (1997): 517–533.

Mukhopadhyay, Carol G. "Moving the Discussion from Race to Racism." *Anthropology Newsletter,* March 1998, 28.

Nakashima, Cynthia L. "An Invisible Monster: The Creation and Denial of Mixed-Race People in America." In Root (1992), 162–178.

Normant, Lynn. "Guess Who's Coming to Dinner Now?: The Sudden Upsurge of Black Women/White Men Celebrity Couples." *Ebony,* September 1992, 48, 50, 52, 144.

O'Crowley, Peggy. "A Matter of Black or White: Debate Swirls Over Interracial Adoption and Cultural Identity." *Sunday Record* (Passaic/ Morris, NJ), 9 April 1995, L1, L14.

O'Hearn, Claudine Chiawei, ed. *Half and Half: Writers on Growing Up Biracial and Bicultural.* New York: Pantheon, 1998.

Omi, Michael, and Howard Winant. *Racial Formation in the United States from the 1960s to the 1980s.* New York: Routledge & Kegan Paul, 1986.

Opitz, May, Katharina Oguntoye, and Dagmar Schultz. *Showing Our Color: Afro-German Women Speak Out.* Amherst: University of Massachusetts Press, 1991.

Overbey, Mary Margaret. "AAA Tells Feds to Eliminate 'Race.'" *Anthropology Newsletter* 38, no. 7 (October 1997): 1, 5.

Page, Helan E. "Understanding White Cultural Practices." *Anthropology Newsletter* 39, no. 1 (April 1998): 60, 58.

Paredes, J. Anthony. "Race Is Not Something You Can See." *Anthropology Newsletter* 38, no. 9 (December 1997): 1, 6.

Parker, Linda Bates. "'My Dad is Black. My Mom is White.'" *Black Collegian* (September/October, 1992): 40, 42.

Perlman, Joel. "Multiracials, Intermarriage, Ethnicity." *Society* 34, no. 6 (1997): 20–24.

Pickard, Heather. "Identity Development in Biracial Children." Salem: Salem State College, November 1996.

Porterfield, Ernest. *Black and White Mixed Marriages*. Chicago: Nelson-Hall, 1978.

Poston, W. S. Carlos. "The Biracial Identity Development Model: A Needed Addition." *Journal of Counseling and Development* 69 (November/December 1990): 152–155.

Prinzing, Fred, and Anita Prinzing. *Mixed Messages*. Chicago: Moody Press, 1991.

Puente, Maria, and Martin Kasindorf. "Blended Races Making a True Melting Pot." *USA Today*, 7 September 1999, 1A, 13A.

Pugh, Clifford. "The Making of Miss Universe." *Texas: Houston Chronicle Magazine*, 30 July 1995, 6–10, 14.

Ragaza, Angelo. "All of the Above: Mixed Race Asian Americans Are Changing the Look and Meaning of Asian American." *A. Magazine* (1994): 21, 22, 76, 77.

Ramirez, Deborah A. "Multiracial Identity in a Color-Conscious World." In Root (1996), 49–62.

Reddy, Maureen T. *Crossing the Color Line: Race, Parenting and Culture*. New Brunswick: Rutgers University Press, 1994.

Reuter, Edward Byron. *The Mulatto in the United States*. Boston: Richard G. Bodger, 1918. Reprint. New York: Johnson Reprint, 1970.

Richardson, Brenda Lane. "Not All Black and White." *Glamour* 90 (August 1992): 252.

Robertson, Tatsha. "Changing Face of the Racial Divide: Mixed Marriages Alter Longtime Boundaries." *Boston Sunday Globe*, 2 January 2000, B1, B8.

Root, Maria P. P., ed. *Racially Mixed People in America*. Newbury Park: Sage Publications, 1992.

———. "The Multicultural Contribution to the Psychological Browning of America." In Zack (1995), 231–236.

———. "A Bill of Rights for Racially Mixed People." In Root (1996), 3–14.

———. *The Multiracial Experience: Racial Borders as the New Frontier*. Thousand Oaks, CA: Sage Publications, 1996.

Rush, Sharon E. "Why Can't You See Her? A Mother Assails Color Blindness in School." *Outlook* 91, no. 4 (Winter 1998): 4–7

Russell, Kathy, Midge Wilson, and Ronald Hall. *The Color Complex: Politics of Skin Color Among African Americans*. New York: Harcourt Brace Jovanovich, 1992.

Samuels, Allison. "Living Color: Multiracial Families Face a Constant Struggle to Fit in Without Denying Part of Their Culture." *Los Angeles Times*, 14 October 1990, E1, E6.

Satris, Stephen. "What Are They?" In Zack (1995), 53–60.

Scales-Trent, Judy. "Commonalities: On Being Black and White, Different and the Same." *Yale Journal of Law and Feminism*, 2, no. 2 (Spring 1990): 305–328.

Schiesel, Seth, and Robert L. Turner. "Is Race Obsolete?: A Move to Change Racial Designations in the US Census Underscores Some Prickly Questions About Who We Are." *Boston Globe Magazine*, 22 September 1996, 12, 15, 16, 19, 20.

Schmidt, Peter. "New Census Policy Could Lead to Major Changes in How Colleges Report Racial Data." *Chronicle of Higher Education*, 14 November 1997, A37.

Schuyler, George S. *Racial Intermarriage in the United States.* Girard: Haldeman-Julius Publications, n.d. [c. 1924–30].

Sege, Irene. "Color Her World: A White Mother of Bi-racial Children Sees Society in a Different Light." *Boston Globe*, 18 January 1995, 23, 28.

———. "Not Black Enough?: Law Professor Heads to BU After Furor at Northwestern Over Her Racial Identity." *Boston Globe*, 9 February 1995, 63, 68.

———. "A Mother's Secret, a Daughter's Search." *Boston Globe*, 2 July 1996, 53, 56–57.

———. "Blending In: Biracial Couples Have Found a Home in a Corner of the US's Whitest State; the Search for Community Goes On." *Boston Globe*, 3 March 1998, E1, E6.

Senna, Danzy. *Caucasia*. New York: Riverhead Books, 1998.

———. "The Mulatto Millenium: Where Will a Former Black Girl Fit?" *Utne Reader* (September/October 1998): 31–32, 34.

Shipman, Pat. "Facing Racial Differences—Together." *Chronicle of Higher Education*, 3 August 1994, B1–3.

Smedley, Audrey. "Origins of 'Race.'" *Anthropology Newsletter* 38, no. 8 (November 1997), 52, 50.

Smith, Patricia. "Love in Black & White." *Boston Sunday Globe*, 23 June 1991, 75, 85.

———. "Is Madison Ave. Whitewashing Blacks?" *Boston Globe*, 14 December 1994, 75, 81.

Smolowe, Jill. "Intermarried with Children." *Time* (Fall 1993): 64–65.

Sollors, Werner. *Neither Black Nor White Yet Both: Thematic Explorations of Interracial Literature.* New York: Oxford University Press, 1997.

———. "'Never Was Born': The Mulatto, An American Tragedy?" *Massachusetts Review* 27, no. 2 (1986): 293–316.

Spencer, Rainier. "Challenge or Collaboration?: Notes from the Struggle Against Racial Categorization." *Interrace Magazine* (October/November 1994): 18–22.

Spickard, Paul R. "The Illogic of American Racial Categories." In Root (1992), 12–23.

————. *Mixed Blood: Intermarriage and Ethnic Identity in Twentieth Century America.* Madison: University of Wisconsin Press, 1989.

Spitzer, Leo. *Lives In Between: Assimilation and Marginality in Austria, Brazil, West Africa, 1780–1945.* Cambridge: Cambridge University Press, 1989.

Stanfield, Rochelle L. "Multiple Choice." *National Journal* 29, no. 47 (November 22, 1997): 2352–2363.

Steel, Melissa. "New Colors: Mixed-Race Families Still Find a Mixed Reception." *Teaching Tolerance* (Spring 1995): 44–49.

Stephan, Cookie White. "Mixed Heritage Individuals: Ethnic Identity and Trait Characteristics." In Root (1996), 50–62.

Stephan, Walter G., and Cookie White Stephan. "Intermarriage: Effects on Personality Adjustment and Intergroup Relations in Two Samples of Students." *Journal of Marriage and the Family* 53 (February 1991): 241–250.

Stevens, Robin. "Growing Up Beige." *Scholastic Update* 121 (April 7, 1989): 9.

Talalay, Kathryn. *Composition in Black and White: the Life of Philippa Schuyler.* New York: Oxford University Press, 1997.

Tatum, Beverly Daniel. *"Why Are All the Black Kids Sitting Together in the Cafeteria?" And Other Conversations About Race.* New York: Basic Books, 1997.

Thomas, Deborah A. "Black, White or Other?" *Essence* (July 1993): 118.

Thomas, Jack. "Charles Austin's Battle of a Lifetime." *Boston Globe*, 7 September 1995, 53, 56–57.

Thompson, Vincent. "Magazine on Multiracial Parenting Launched." *Philadelphia Tribune*, 1 March 1994, 1B, 2B.

Thornton, Michael C. "Hidden Agendas, Identity Theories and Multiracial People." In Root (1996), 101–120.

Tilove, Jonathon. "Biracial Couples Find America is More Tolerant Than It Knows." *Star-Ledger* (Trenton NJ), 21 June 1991, 22.

Tucker, M. Belinda, and Claudia Mitchell-Kernan. "New Trends in Black American Interracial Marriage: The Social Structural Context." *Journal of Marriage and the Family* 52 (1990): 209–218.

Turner, Victor. *The Forest of Symbols.* Ithaca: Cornell University Press, 1967.

Updike, David. "The Colorings of Childhood: On the Burdens, and Privileges, Facing my Multiracial Son." *Harper's Magazine* 284 (January 1992): 63–67.

van Gennep, Arnold. *The Rites of Passage.* Chicago: University of Chicago Press, 1960.

Waldron, Jan L. *Giving Away Simone.* New York: Times Book, 1995.

Walker, Rebecca. "Lusting for Freedom." In *Listen Up: Voices from the Next Feminist Generation*, edited by Barbara Findlen, 95–101. Seattle: Seal Press, 1995.

Wheeler, David L. "Helping Mixed-Race People Declare Their Heritage." *Chronicle of Higher Education*, 7 September 1994, A8.

———. "Black Children, White Parents: The Difficult Issue of Transracial Adoption." *Chronicle of Higher Education*, 15 September 1993, A8, A9, A16.

White, Jack. "*'I'm Just Who I Am': Race Is No Longer As Simple As Black or White. So, What Does This Mean for America?*" *Time* 149, no. 18 (May 5,1997): 32–34.

Wiggins, Cynthia. "Anomalous Like Me." *Washington Post*, 3 May 1998, F1, F8.

Wijeyesinghe, Charmaine L. "Understanding and Responding to the Racial Identity Development of Multiracial Students." Paper presented at seventh annual National Conference on Race and Ethnicity in American Higher Education, Atlanta, GA, June 1994.

Williams, Gregory Howard. *Life on the Color Line: The True Story of a White Boy Who Discovered He Was Black*. New York: Dutton, 1995.

Williams, Teresa Kay. "Prism Lives: Identity of Binational Amerasians." In Root (1992), 280–307.

———. "Race as Process: Reassessing the 'What Are You?' Encounters of Biracial Individuals." In Root (1996), 191–210.

Williamson, Joel. *New People: Miscegenation and Mulattoes in the United States*. New York: The Free Press, 1980.

Wilson, Barbara Foley. "Marriage's Melting Pot." *American Demographics* 6 (July 1984): 34–37, 45.

Winkler, Karen J. "Scholars Explore the Blurred Lines of Race, Gender, and Ethnicity: Research Examines How People Move from One Category to Another or Blend Them." *Chronicle of Higher Education*, 11 July 1997, A 11–12.

Wood, Joe. "Fade to Black: Once Upon a Time in Multiracial America." *Village Voice* 39, no. 49 (December 6, 1994): 25–26, 28–34.

Wright, Lawrence. "One Drop of Blood." *New Yorker*, 25 July 1994, 46–55.

———. "Double Mystery." *New Yorker*, 7 August 1995, 45–62.

Yemma, John. "Race Debate Simmers Over Who Is What." *Boston Sunday Globe*, 11 May 1997, A1, A30.

———. "'Whiteness Studies' an Attempt at Healing." *Boston Sunday Globe*, 21 December 1997, A1, A40.

Zack, Naomi, ed. *American Mixed Race: The Culture of Microdiversity*. Lanham, MD: Rowman and Littlefield Publishers, 1995.

———. *Race and Mixed Race*. Philadelphia: Temple University Press, 1993.

Index

About the Author

MARION KILSON is Dean of the Graduate School, Salem State College, Massachusetts.